Marx Joyce
Abbott Hardy Montaigne Machiavelli Chesterton Cooper Emerson Austen
Defoe Melville Haggard Hugo
Carroll Christie Eliot Grimm
Stoker Molière
Wilde Maupassant Byron
Einstein Fitzgerald Engels Schiller
Garnett Smith
Goethe Hawthorne Kafka
Dostoyevsky
Cotton Kipling Doyle Hall
Baum Willis
Leslie Dumas Henry Nietzsche
Flaubert Turgenev Balzac
Stockton Vatsyayana Crane
Burroughs Verne
Curtis Tocqueville Whitman Gogol Vinci
Homer Widger Tolstoy Busch
Darwin Thoreau
Potter Freud Zola Twain Plato Scott
Lawrence
Kant Jowett Stevenson Dickens
Andersen Cervantes Burton Hesse Harte
London Descartes
Poe Aristotle Wells Voltaire
Hale James Hastings Cooke
Bunner Shakespeare
Richter Chambers Irving
Chekhov da Shaw Wodehouse Benedict
Doré Swift Dante Alcott
Pushkin
Newton

tredition

tredition was established in 2006 by Sandra Latusseck and Soenke Schulz. Based in Hamburg, Germany, tredition offers publishing solutions to authors and publishing houses, combined with worldwide distribution of printed and digital book content. tredition is uniquely positioned to enable authors and publishing houses to create books on their own terms and without conventional manufacturing risks.

For more information please visit: www.tredition.com

TREDITION CLASSICS

This book is part of the TREDITION CLASSICS series. The creators of this series are united by passion for literature and driven by the intention of making all public domain books available in printed format again - worldwide. Most TREDITION CLASSICS titles have been out of print and off the bookstore shelves for decades. At tredition we believe that a great book never goes out of style and that its value is eternal. Several mostly non-profit literature projects provide content to tredition. To support their good work, tredition donates a portion of the proceeds from each sold copy. As a reader of a TREDITION CLASSICS book, you support our mission to save many of the amazing works of world literature from oblivion. See all available books at www.tredition.com.

Project Gutenberg

The content for this book has been graciously provided by Project Gutenberg. Project Gutenberg is a non-profit organization founded by Michael Hart in 1971 at the University of Illinois. The mission of Project Gutenberg is simple: To encourage the creation and distribution of eBooks. Project Gutenberg is the first and largest collection of public domain eBooks.

The Substance of a Journal During a Residence at the Red River Colony, British North America and Frequent Excursions Among the North-West American Indians, In the Years 1820, 1821, 1822, 1823.

John West

Imprint

This book is part of TREDITION CLASSICS

Author: John West
Cover design: Buchgut, Berlin – Germany

Publisher: tredition GmbH, Hamburg - Germany
ISBN: 978-3-8472-3926-0

www.tredition.com
www.tredition.de

The intention of the TREDITION CLASSICS series is to make world literature in the public domain available in printed format. Literary enthusiasts and organizations, such as Project Gutenberg, worldwide have scanned and digitally edited the original texts. tredition has subsequently formatted and redesigned the content into a modern reading layout. Therefore, we cannot guarantee the exact reproduction of the original format of a particular historic edition. Please also note that no modifications have been made to the spelling, therefore it may differ from the orthography used today.

PREFACE.

We live in a day when the most distant parts of the earth are opening as the sphere of Missionary labours. The state of the heathen world is becoming better known, and the sympathy of British Christians has been awakened, in zealous endeavours to evangelize and soothe its sorrows. In these encouraging signs of the times, the Author is induced to give the following pages to the public, from having traversed some of the dreary wilds of North America, and felt deeply interested in the religious instruction and amelioration of the condition of the natives. They are wandering, in unnumbered tribes, through vast wildernesses, where generation after generation have passed away, in gross ignorance and almost brutal degradation.

Should any information he is enabled to give excite a further Christian sympathy, and more active benevolence in their behalf, it will truly rejoice his heart: and his prayer to God, is, that the Aborigines of a British Territory, may not remain as outcasts from British Missionary exertions; but may be raised through their instrumentality, to what they are capable of enjoying, the advantages of civilized and social life, with the blessings of Christianity.

September, 1824.

CONTENTS.

THE RED RIVER COLONY; AND THE NORTH-WEST-AMERICAN INDIANS.

CHAPTER I.

DEPARTURE FROM ENGLAND. ARRIVAL AT THE ORKNEY ISLES. ENTER HUDSON'S STRAITS. ICEBERGS. ESQUIMAUX. KILLING A POLAR BEAR. YORK FACTORY. EMBARKED FOR THE RED RIVER COLONY. DIFFICULTIES OF THE NAVIGATION. LAKE WINIPEG. MUSKEGGOWUCK, OR SWAMP INDIANS. PIGEWIS, A CHIEF OF THE CHIPPEWAYS OR SALTEAUX TRIBE. ARRIVAL AT THE RED RIVER. COLONISTS. SCHOOL ESTABLISHED. WOLF-DOGS. INDIANS VISIT FORT DOUGLAS. DESIGN OF A BUILDING FOR DIVINE WORSHIP.

On the 27th of May, 1820, I embarked at Gravesend, on board the Honourable Hudson's Bay Company's ship, the Eddystone; accompanied by the ship, Prince of Wales, and the Luna brig, for Hudson's Bay. In my appointment as Chaplain to the Company, my instructions were, to reside at the Red River Settlement, and under the encouragement and aid of the Church Missionary Society, I was to seek the instruction, and endeavour to meliorate the condition of the native Indians.

The anchor was weighed early on the following morning, and sailing with a fine breeze, the sea soon opened to our view. The thought that I was now leaving all that was dear to me upon earth, to encounter the perils of the ocean, and the wilderness, sensibly affected me at times; but my feelings were relieved in the sanguine hope that I was borne on my way under the guidance of a kind protecting Providence, and that the circumstances of the country whither I was bound, would soon admit of my being surrounded with my family. With these sentiments, I saw point after point sink in the horizon, as we passed the shores of England and Scotland for the Orkneys.

We bore up for these Isles on the 10th of June, after experiencing faint and variable winds for several days: and a more dreary scene can scarcely be imagined than they present to the eye, in general. No tree or shrub is visible; and all is barren except a few spots of cultivated ground in the vales, which form a striking contrast with the barren heath-covered hills that surround them. These cultivated spots mark the residence of the hardy Orkneyman in a wretched looking habitation with scarcely any other light, (as I found upon landing on one of the islands) than from a smoke hole, or from an aperture in the wall, closed at night with a tuft of grass. The calf and pig were seen as inmates, while the little furniture that appeared, was either festooned with strings of dried fish, or crossed with a perch for the fowls to roost on.

A different scene, however, presented itself, as we anchored the next day in the commodious harbour of Stromness. The view of the town, with the surrounding cultivated parts of the country, and the Hoy Hill, is striking and romantic, and as our stay here was for a few days, I accepted an invitation to the Manse, from the kind and worthy minister of Hoy, and ascended with him the hill, of about 1620 feet high.

The sabbath we spent at sea was a delight to me, from the arrangement made by the captain for the attendance of the passengers and part of the crew on divine worship, both morning and afternoon. Another sabbath had now returned, and the weather being fair, all were summoned to attend on the quarter deck. We commenced the service by singing the Old Hundredth Psalm, and our voices being heard by the crews of several ships, lying near to us at anchor, they were seen hurrying on deck from below, so as to present to us a most interesting and gratifying sight—

""We stood, and under open sky adored

The God, that made both 'seas,' air, earth, and heaven.""

There appeared to be a solemn impression; and I trust that religion was felt among us as a divine reality.

June 22.—The ships got under weigh to proceed on our voyage; and as we passed the rugged and broken rocks of Hoy Head, we were reminded of the fury of a tempestuous ocean, in forming some of them into detached pillars, and vast caverns; while they left an impression upon the mind, of desolation and danger. We had not sailed more than one hundred miles on the Atlantic before it blew a strong head wind, and several on board with myself were greatly affected by the motion of the ship. It threw me into such a state of languor, that I felt as though I could have willingly yielded to have been cast overboard, and it was nearly a week before I was relieved from this painful sensation and nausea, peculiar to sea sickness.

Without any occurrence worthy of notice we arrived in Davis's Straits on the 19th of July, where Greenland ships are sometimes met with, returning from the whale fishery, but we saw not a single whaler in this solitary part of the ocean. The Mallemuk, found in great numbers off Greenland, and the ""Larus crepidatus,"" or black toed gull, frequently visited us; and for nearly a whole day, a large shoal of the ""Delphinus deductor,"" or leading whale, was observed following the ship. The captain ordered the harpoons and lances to be in readiness in case we fell in with the great Greenland whale, but nothing was seen of this monster of the deep.

In approaching Hudson's straits, we first saw one of those beautiful features in the scenery of the North, an Iceberg, which being driven with vast masses of ice off Cape Farewell, South Greenland, are soon destroyed by means of the solar heat, and tempestuous force of the sea. The thermometer was at 27°#176; on the night of the 22nd, with ice in the boat; and in the afternoon we saw an ice-blink, a beautiful effulgence or reflection of light over the floating ice, to the extent of forty or fifty miles. The next day we passed Resolution Island, Lat. 61°#176; 25', Long. 65°#176; 2' and all was desolate and inhospitable in the view over black barren rocks, and in the aspect of the shore. This being Sunday, I preached in the morning, catechized the young people in the afternoon, and had divine service again in the evening, as was our custom every sabbath in crossing the Atlantic, when the weather would permit: and it afforded me much pleasure to witness the sailors at times in groups reading the life of Newton, or some religious tracts which I put into their hands. The Scotch I found generally well and scripturally informed, and several of them joined the young people in reading to me the New Testatament, and answering the catechetical questions. In our passage through the Straits, our progress was impeded by vast fields of ice, and icebergs floating past us in every form of desolate magnificence. The scene was truly grand and impressive, and mocks imagination to describe. There is a solemn and an overwhelming sensation produced in the mind, by these enormous masses of snow and ice, not to be conveyed in words. They floated by us from one to two hundred feet above the water, and sometimes of great length, resembling huge mountains, with deep vallies between, lofty cliffs, and all the imposing objects in nature, passing in silent grandeur, except at intervals, when the fall of one was heard, or the crashing of the ice struck the ear like the noise of distant thunder.

When nearly off Saddle Back, with a light favourable breeze, and about ten miles from the shore, the Esquimaux who, visit the Straits during summer, were observed with their one man skin canoes, followed by women in some of a larger size, paddling towards the ship. No sooner was the sail shortened than we were surrounded by nearly two hundred of them: the men raising their paddles as they approached us, shouting with much exultation, 'chimo! chimo! pillattaa! pillattaa!' expressions probably of friendship, or trade. They were particularly eager to exchange all that they apparently possessed, and hastily bartered with the Eddystone, blubber, whalebone, and seahorse teeth, for axes, saws, knives, tin kettles, and bits of old iron hoop. The women presented image toys, made from the bones and teeth of animals, models of canoes, and various articles of dress, made of seal skins, and the membranes of the abdomen of the whale, all of which displayed considerable ingenuity and neatness, and for which they received in exchange, needles, knives, and beads. It was very clear that European deception had reached them, from the manner in which they *tenaciously* held their articles till they *grasped* what was offered in barter for them; and immediately they got the merchandise in possession, they licked it with their tongues, in satisfaction that it was their own. The tribe appeared to be well-conditioned in their savage state, and remarkably healthy. Some of the children, I observed, were eating raw flesh, from the bones of animals that had been killed, and given them by their mothers, who appeared to have a strong natural affection for their offspring. I threw one of them a halfpenny, which she caught; and pointing to the child she immediately gave it to him with much apparent fondness. It has been supposed that in holding up their children, as is sometimes the case, it is for barter, but I should rather conclude that it is for the purpose of exciting commiseration, and to obtain some European article for them. A few of the men were permitted to come on board, and the good humour of the captain invited one to dance with him: he took the step with much agility and quickness, and imitated every gesture of his lively partner. The breeze freshening, we soon parted with this barbarous people, and when at a short distance from the ship, they assembled in their canoes, each taking hold of the adjoining one, in apparent consultation, as to what bargains they had made, and what articles they possessed, till a canoe was observed to break off from the group, which they all followed for their haunts along the shores of Terra Neiva, and the Savage Islands. Having a copy of the Esquimaux Gospels from the British and Foreign Bible Society, it was my wish to have read part of a chapter to them, with a view to ascertain, if possible, whether they knew of the Moravian Missionary establishment at Nain, on the Labrador coast; but such was the haste, bustle, and noise of their intercourse with us, that I lost the opportunity. Though they have exchanged articles in barter for many years, it is not known whether they are from the Labrador shore on a summer excursion for killing seals, and the whale fishery, or from the East main coast, where they return and winter.

The highest point of latitude we reached in our course, was 62°#176; 44'—longitude 74°#176; 16', and when off Cape Digges we parted company with the Prince of Wales, as bound to James's Bay. We stood on direct for York Factory, and when about fifty miles from Cary Swan's Nest, the chief mate pointed out to me a polar bear, with her two cubs swimming towards the ship. He immediately ordered the jolly-boat to be lowered, and asked me to accompany him in the attempt to kill her. Some axes were put into the boat, in case the ferocious animal should approach us in the attack; and the sailors pulled away in the direction she was swimming. At the first shot, when within about one hundred yards, she growled tremendously, and immediately made for the boat; but having the advantage in rowing faster than she could swim, our guns were reloaded till she was killed, and one of the cubs also accidentally, from swimming close to the mother; the other got upon the floating carcase, and was towed to the side of the ship, when a noose was put around its neck, and it was hauled on board for the captain to take with him alive, on his return to England.

August 3.—We fell in with a great deal of floating ice, the weather was very foggy, and the thermometer at freezing point. The ship occasionally received some heavy blows, and with difficulty made way along a vein of water. On the 5th we were completely blocked in with ice, and nothing was to be seen in every part of the horizon, but one vast mass, as a barrier to our proceeding. It was a terrific, and sublime spectacle; and the human mind cannot conceive any thing more awful, than the destruction of a ship, by the meeting of two enormous fields of ice, advancing against each other at the rate of several miles an hour. ""It may easily be imagined,"" says Captain Scoresby, ""that the strongest ship can no more withstand the shock of the contact of two fields, than a sheet of paper can stop a musket-ball. Numbers of vessels since the establishment of the Whale Fishery have been thus destroyed. Some have been thrown upon the ice. Some have had their hulls completely thrown open, and others have been buried beneath the heaped fragments of the ice.""—

Sunday, the 6th.—Text in the morning 1st book Samuel, 30th chapter, latter part of the 6th verse. The weather was very variable, with much thunder and lightening; which was awful and impressive. On the 12th the thermometer was below freezing point, and the rigging of the ship was covered with large icicles. Intense fogs often prevailed, but of very inconsiderable height. They would sometimes obscure the hull of the ship, when the mast head was seen, and the sun was visible and effulgent.

In the evening of the 13th, the sailors gave three cheers, as we got under weigh on the opening of the ice by a strong northerly wind, and left the vast mass which had jammed us in for many days. The next day we saw the land, and came to the anchorage at York Flatts the following morning, with sentiments of gratitude to God for his protecting Providence through the perils of the ice and of the sea, and for the little interruption in the duties of my profession from the state of the weather, during the voyage.

I was kindly received by the Governor at the Factory, the principal depôt of the Hudson's Bay Company, and on the sabbath, every arrangement was made for the attendance of the Company's servants on divine worship, both parts of the day. Observing a number of half-breed children running about, growing up in ignorance and idleness; and being informed that they were a numerous offspring of Europeans by Indian women, and found at all the Company's Posts; I drew up a plan, which I submitted to the Governor, for collecting a certain number of them, to be maintained, clothed, and educated upon a regularly organized system. It was transmitted by him to the Committee of the Hudson's Bay Company, whose benevolent feelings towards this neglected race, had induced them to send several schoolmasters to the country, fifteen or sixteen years ago; but who were unhappily diverted from their original purpose, and became engaged as fur traders.

During my stay at this post, I visited several Indian families, and no sooner saw them crowded together in their miserable-looking tents, than I felt a lively interest (as I anticipated) in their behalf. Unlike the Esquimaux I had seen in Hudson's Straits, with their flat, fat, greasy faces, these '*Swampy Crees*' presented a way-worn countenance, which depicted ""Suffering without comfort, while they sunk without hope."" The contrast was striking, and forcibly impressed my mind with the idea, that Indians who knew not the corrupt influence and barter of spirituous liquors at a Trading Post, were far happier, than the wretched-looking group around me. The duty devolved upon me, to seek to meliorate their sad condition, as degraded and emaciated, wandering in ignorance, and wearing away a short existence in one continued succession of hardships in procuring food. I was told of difficulties, and some spoke of impossibilities in the way of teaching them Christianity or the first rudiments of settled and civilized life; but with a combination of opposing circumstances, I determined not to be intimidated, nor to ""confer with flesh and blood,"" but to put my hand immediately to the plough, in the attempt to break in upon this heathen wilderness. If little hope could be cherished of the adult Indian in his wandering and unsettled habits of life, it appeared to me, that a *wide* and *most extensive field*, presented itself for cultivation in the instruction of the native children. With the aid of an interpreter, I spoke to an Indian, called Withaweecapo, about taking two of his boys to the Red River Colony with me to educate and maintain. He yielded to my request; and I shall never forget the affectionate manner in which he brought the eldest boy in his arms, and placed him in the canoe on the morning of my departure from York Factory. His two wives, sisters, accompanied him to the water's edge, and while they stood gazing on us, as the canoe was paddled from the shore, I considered that I bore a pledge from the Indian that many more children might be found, if an establishment were formed in British Christian sympathy, and British liberality for their education and support.

I had to establish the principle, that the North-American Indian of these regions would part with his children, to be educated in white man's knowledge and religion. The above circumstance therefore afforded us no small encouragement, in embarking for the colony. We overtook the boats going thither on the 7th of September, slowly proceeding through a most difficult and laborious navigation. The men were harnessed to a line, as they walked along the steep declivity of a high bank, dragging them against a strong current. In many places, as we proceeded, the water was very shoal, and opposed us with so much force in the rapids, that the men were frequently obliged to get out, and lift the boats over the stones; at other times to unload, and launch them over the rocks, and carry the goods upon their backs, or rather suspended in slings from their heads, a considerable distance, over some of the portages. The weather was frequently very cold, with snow and rain; and our progress was so slow and mortifying, particularly up Hill River, that the boats' crews were heard to execrate the man who first found out such a way into the interior.

The blasphemy of the men, in the difficulties they had to encounter, was truly painful to me. I had hoped better things of the Scotch, from their known moral and enlightened education; but their horrid imprecations proved a degeneracy of character in an Indian country. This I lamented to find was too generally the case with Europeans, particularly so in their barbarous treatment of women. They do not admit them as their companions, nor do they allow them to eat at their tables, but degrade them *merely* as slaves to their arbitrary inclinations; while the children grow up wild and uncultivated as the heathen.

The scenery throughout the passage is dull and monotonous (excepting a few points in some of the small lakes, which are picturesque), till you reach the Company's post, Norway House; when a fine body of water bursts upon your view in Lake Winipeg. We found the voyage, from the Factory to this point, so sombre and dreary, that the sight of a horse grazing on the bank greatly exhilarated us, in the association of the idea that we were approaching some human habitation. Our provisions being short, we recruited our stock at this post; and I obtained another boy for education, reported to me as the orphan son of a deceased Indian and a half-caste woman; and taught him the prayer which the other used morning and evening, and which he soon learned:—""*Great Father, bless me, through Jesus Christ.*"" May a gracious God hear their cry, and raise them up as heralds of his salvation in this truly benighted and barbarous part of the world.

It often grieved me, in our hurried passage, to see the men employed in taking the goods over the carrying places, or in rowing, during the Sabbath. I contemplated the delight with which thousands in England enjoyed the privileges of this sacred day, and welcomed divine ordinances. In reading, meditation, and prayer, however, my soul was not forsaken of God, and I gladly embraced an opportunity of calling those more immediately around me to join in reading the scriptures, and in prayer in my tent.

October the 6th. The ground was covered with snow, and the weather most winterly, when we embarked in our open boats to cross the lake for the Red River. Its length, from north to south, is about three hundred miles; and it abounds with sunken rocks, which are very dangerous to boats sailing in a fresh breeze. It is usual to run along shore, for the sake of an encampment at night, and of getting into a creek for shelter, in ease of storms and tempestuous weather. We had run about half the lake, when the boat, under a press of sail, struck upon one of these rocks, with so much violence as to threaten our immediate destruction. The idea of never more seeing my family upon earth, rushed upon my mind; but the pang of thought was alleviated by the recollection that life at best was short, and that they would soon meet me in 'brighter worlds,' whither I expected to be hurried, through the supposed hasty death of drowning. Providentially however we escaped being wrecked; and I could not but bless the God of my salvation, for the anchor of hope afforded me amidst all dangers and difficulties and possible privations of life.

As I sat at the door of my tent near a fire one evening, an Indian joined me, and gave me to understand that he knew a little English. He told me that he was taken prisoner when very young, and subsequently fell into the hands of an American gentleman, who took him to England, where he was very much frightened lest the houses should fall upon him. He further added that he knew a little of Jesus Christ, and hoped that I would teach him to read, when he came to the Red River, which he intended to do after he had been on a visit to his relations. He has a most interesting intelligent countenance, and expressed much delight at my coming over to his country to teach the Indians. We saw but few of them in our route along the courses of the river, and on the banks of the Winipeg. These are called Muskeggouck, or Swamp Indians, and are considered a distinct tribe, between the Nahathaway or Cree and Saulteaux. They subsist on fish, and occasionally the moose deer or elk, with the rein deer or caribou, vast numbers of which, as they swim the river in spring and in the fall of the year, the Indians spear in their canoes. In times of extremity they gather moss from the rocks, that is called by the Canadians 'tripe de roche,' which boils into a clammy substance, and has something of a nutritious quality. The general appearance of these Indians is that of wretchedness and want, and excited in my mind much sympathy towards them. I shook hands with them, in the hope that ere the rising generation at least had passed away, the light of Christianity, like the *aurora borealis* relieving the gloom of their winter night, would shed around them its heavenly lustre, and cheer their suffering existence with a scriptural hope of immortality.

In crossing the Winipeg, we saw almost daily large flocks of wild fowl, geese, ducks, and swans, flying to the south; which was a sure indication to us that winter was setting in with severity to the north. In fact it had already visited us, and inflicted much suffering from cold; and it was with no small delight that we entered the mouth of Red River, soon after the sun rose in majestic splendour over the lake, on the morning of the 13th of October. We proceeded to Netley Creek to breakfast, where we met Pigewis the chief of a tribe of Saulteaux Indians, who live principally along the banks of the river. This chief breakfasted with the party, and shaking hands with me most cordially, expressed a wish that ""more of the stumps and brushwood were cleared away for my feet, in coming to see his country."" On our apprising him of the Earl of Selkirk's death, he expressed much sorrow, and appeared to feel deeply the loss which he and the colony had sustained in his Lordship's decease. He shewed me the following high testimony of his character, given him by the late Earl when at Red River.

""The bearer, Pigewis, one of the principal chiefs of the Chipewyans, or Saulteaux of Red River, has been a steady friend of the settlement ever since its first establishment, and has never deserted its cause in its greatest reverses. He has often exerted his influence to restore peace; and having rendered most essential services to the settlers in their distress, deserves to be treated with favour and distinction by the officers of the Hudson's Bay Company, and by all the friends of peace and good order.""

(Signed.)SELKIRK.

Fort Douglas, July 17, 1820.

As we proceeded, the banks were covered with oak, elm, ash, poplar, and maple, and rose gradually higher as we approached the Colony, when the praries, or open grassy plains, presented to the eye an agreeable contrast with the almost continued forest of pine we were accustomed to in the route from York Factory. On the 14th of October we reached the settlement, consisting of a number of huts widely scattered along the margin of the river; in vain did I look for a cluster of cottages, where the hum of a small population at least might be heard as in a village. I saw but few marks of human industry in the cultivation of the soil. Almost every inhabitant we passed bore a gun upon his shoulder and all appeared in a wild and hunter-like state. The colonists were a compound of individuals of various countries. They were principally Canadians, and Germans of the Meuron regiment; who were discharged in Canada at the conclusion of the American war, and were mostly Catholics. There was a large population of Scotch emigrants also, who with some retired servants of the Hudson's Bay Company were chiefly Protestants, and by far the most industrious in agricultural pursuits. There was an unfinished building as a Catholic church, and a small house adjoining, the residence of the Priest; but no Protestant manse, church, or school house, which obliged me to take up my abode at the Colony Fort, (Fort Douglas,) where the 'Chargè d'Affaires' of the settlement resided; and who kindly afforded the accommodation of a room for divine worship on the sabbath. My ministry was generally well attended by the settlers; and soon after my arrival I got a log-house repaired about three miles below the Fort, among the Scotch population, where the schoolmaster took up his abode, and began teaching from twenty to twenty-five of the children.

Nov. the 8th.—The river was frozen over, and the winter set in with severity. Many were harnessing and trying their dogs in sledges, with a view to *trip* to Pembina, a distance of about seventy miles, or to the Hunters' tents, on the plains, for buffaloe meat. The journey generally takes them a fortnight, or sometimes more, before they return to the settlement with provisions; and this rambling and uncertain mode of obtaining subsistence in their necessity, (the locusts having then destroyed their crops,) has given the settlers a fondness for *tripping*, to the neglect of improving their dwellings and their farms. The dogs used on these occasions, and for travelling in carioles over the snow, strongly resemble the wolf in size, and frequently in colour. They have pointed noses, small sharp ears, long bushy tails, and a savage aspect. They never bark, but set up a fierce growl, and when numerous about a Fort, their howling is truly melancholy. A doubt can no longer exist, that the dogs brought to the interior of these wilds by Europeans, engendered with the wolf, and produced these dogs in common use. They have no attachment, and destroy all domestic animals. They are lashed to a sledge, and are often *brutally* driven to travel thirty or forty miles a day, dragging after them a load of three and four hundred pounds weight. When fat, they are eaten by the Canadians as a great delicacy; and are generally presented by the Indians at their feasts.

Many Indian families came frequently to the Fort, and as is common, I believe, to all the aborigines were of a copper colour complexion, with black coarse hair. Whenever they dressed for any particular occasion, they anointed themselves all over with charcoal and grease, and painted their eyebrows, lips and forehead, or cheeks, with vermillion. Some had their noses perforated through the cartilage, in which was fixed part of a goose quill, or a piece of tin, worn as an ornament, while others strutted with the skin of a raven ingeniously folded as a head dress, to present the beak over the forehead, and the tail spreading over the back of the neck. Their clothing consisted principally of a blanket, a buffaloe skin, and leggings, with a cap, which hung down their back, and was fastened to a belt round the waist. *Scoutaywaubo*, or fire water, (rum) was their principal request; to obtain which they appeared ready to barter any thing, or every thing they possessed. The children ran about almost naked, and were treated by their parents with all the instinctive fondness of animals. They know of no restraint, and as they grow up into life, they are left at full liberty to be absolute masters of their own actions. They were very lively, and several of them had pleasing countenances which indicated a capacity for much intellectual improvement. Most of their ears were cut in large holes, to which were suspended various ornaments, but principally those of beads. Their mothers were in the practice of some disgusting habits towards them particularly that of devouring the vermin which were engendered from their dirty heads. They put into their mouths all that they happen to find, and will sometimes reserve a quantity, and present the choice collection as a *bonne bouche* to their husbands.

After a short stay at the settlement, they left us to roam through the forests, like animals, without any fixed residence, in search of provisions, till the rivers open in the following spring, when they return to the Company's Post, and trade with the skins and furs which they have taken in hunting.

December the 6th. My residence was now removed to the farm belonging to the late Earl of Selkirk, about three miles from Fort Douglas, and six from the school. Though more comfortable in my quarters, than at the Fort, the distance put me to much inconvenience in my professional duties. We continued, however, to have divine service regularly on the Sabbath; and having frequently enforced the moral, and social obligation of marriage upon those who were living with, and had families by Indian, or half caste women, I had the happiness to perform the ceremony for several of the most respectable of the settlers, under the conviction, that *the institution of marriage, and the security of property, were the fundamental laws of society*. I had also many baptisms; and with infants, some adult half-breeds were brought to be baptized. I endeavoured to explain to them simply and faithfully the nature and object of that Divine ordinance; but found great difficulty in conveying to their minds any just and true ideas of the Saviour, who gave the commission, on his ascension into heaven ""To go and teach all nations, baptizing them in the name of the Father, and of the Son, and of the Holy Ghost."" This difficulty produced in me a strong desire to extend the blessing of education to them: and from this period it became a leading object with me, to erect in a central situation, a substantial building, which should contain apartments for the school-master, afford accommodation for Indian children, be a day-school for the children of the settlers, enable us to establish a Sunday school for the half-caste adult population who would attend, and fully answer the purpose of a church for the present, till a brighter prospect arose in the colony, and its inhabitants were more congregated. I became anxious to see such a building arise as a Protestant land-mark of Christianity in a vast field of heathenism and general depravity of manners, and cheerfully gave my hand and my heart to perfect the work. I expected a willing co-operation from the Scotch settlers; but was disappointed in my sanguine hopes of their cheerful and persevering assistance, through their prejudices against the English Liturgy, and the simple rites of our communion. I visited them however in their affliction, and performed all ministerial duties as their Pastor; while my motto, was—Perseverance.

CHAPTER II.

VISIT THE SCHOOL. LEAVE THE FORKS FOR QU'APPELLE. ARRIVAL AT BRANDON HOUSE. INDIAN CORPSE STAGED. MARRIAGES AT COMPANY'S POST. BAPTISMS. DISTRIBUTION OF THE SCRIPTURES. DEPARTURE FROM BRANDON HOUSE. ENCAMPMENT. ARRIVAL AT QU'APPELLE. CHARACTER AND CUSTOMS OF STONE INDIANS. STOP AT SOME HUNTERS' TENTS ON RETURN TO THE COLONY. VISIT PEMBINA. HUNTING BUFFALOES. INDIAN ADDRESS. CANADIAN VOYAGEURS. INDIAN MARRIAGES. BURIAL GROUND. PEMICAN. INDIAN HUNTER SENDS HIS SON TO BE EDUCATED. MOSQUITOES. LOCUSTS.

January 1, 1821.—I went to the school this morning, a distance of about six miles from my residence, to examine the children, and was much pleased at the progress which they had already made in reading. Having addressed them, and prayed for a divine blessing on their instruction: I distributed to those who could read a little book, as a reward for their general good conduct in the school. In returning to the farm, my mind was filled with sentiments of gratitude and love to a divine Saviour for his providential protection, and gracious favour towards me during the past year. He has shielded me in the shadow of his hand through the perils of the sea and of the wilderness from whence I may derive motives of devotion and activity in my profession. Thousands are involved in worse than Egyptian darkness around me, wandering in ignorance and perishing through lack of knowledge. When will this wide waste howling wilderness blossom as the rose, and the desert become as a fruitful field! Generations *may* first pass away; and the seed of instruction that is now sown, may lie buried, waiting for the early and the latter rain, yet, the sure word of Prophecy, will ever animate Christian liberality and exertion, in the bright prospect of that glorious period, when Christianity shall burst upon the gloomy scene of heathenism, and dispel every cloud of ignorance and superstition, till *the very ends of the earth* shall see the salvation of the Lord.

As I returned from divine service at the Fort, to the farm, on the 7th, it rained hard for nearly two hours, which is a very unusual thing during winter in this northern latitude. We have seldom any rain for nearly six months, but a continued hard frost the greater part of this period. The sky is generally clear, and the snow lies about fifteen, or at the utmost eighteen inches deep. As the climate of a country is not known by merely measuring its distance from the equator, but is affected differently in the same parallel of latitude by its locality, and a variety of circumstances, we find that of Red River, though situated in the same parallel, far different from, and intensely more cold than, that of England. The thermometer is frequently at 30°#176; and 40°#176; below zero, when it is only about freezing point in the latter place. This difference is probably occasioned by the prevailing north-westerly wind, that blows with piercing keenness over the rocky mountains, or Andes, which run from north to south through the whole Continent, and over a country which is buried in ice and snow.

As my instructions were to afford religious instruction and consolation to the servants in the active employment of the Hudson's Bay Company, as well as to the Company's retired servants, and other inhabitants of the settlement, upon such occasions as the nature of the country and other circumstances would permit; I left the Forks[1] in a cariole drawn by three dogs, accompanied by a sledge with two dogs, to carry the luggage and provisions, and two men as drivers, on the 15th of January, for Brandon House, and Qu'appelle, on the Assiniboine River. After we had travelled about fifteen miles, we stopped on the edge of a wood, and *bivouacked* on the snow for the night. A large fire was soon kindled, and a supply of wood cut to keep it up; when supper being prepared and finished, I wrapped myself in my blankets and buffaloe robe, and laid down with a few twigs under me in place of a bed, with my feet towards the fire, and slept soundly under the open canopy of heaven. The next morning we left our encampment before sunrise; and the country as we passed presented some beautiful points and bluffs of wood. We started again early the following morning, which was intensely cold; and I had much difficulty in keeping my face from freezing, on my way to the encampment rather late in the evening, at the '*Portage de Prairè*.' In crossing the plain the next morning, with a sharp head wind, my nose and part of my face were frozen quite hard and white. I was not conscious of it, till it was perceived by the driver, who immediately rubbed the parts affected well with snow, and restored the circulation, so that I suffered no inconvenience from the circumstance, but was obliged to keep my face covered with a blanket as I lay in the cariole the remaining part of the day.

On the 19th we were on the march as early as half past four, and had a sharp piercing wind in our faces, which drifted the snow, and made the track very bad for the dogs. This greatly impeded our progress; and our provisions being short, I shot some ptarmigans, which were frequently seen on our route. We perceived some traces of the buffaloe, and the wolf was frequently seen following our track, or crossing in the line we were travelling. Jan. 20. We started at sunrise, with a very cold head wind; and my favourite English watch dog, Neptune, left the encampment, to follow us, with great reluctance. I was apprehensive that he might turn back, on account of the severity of the morning; and being obliged to put my head under the blanket in the cariole, I requested the driver to encourage him along. We had not pursued our journey however more than an hour, before I was grieved to find that the piercing keenness of the wind had forced him to return; and the poor animal was probably soon after devoured by the wolves.

We arrived at Brandon House, the Company's provision post, about three o'clock; and the next day, being Sunday, the servants were all assembled for divine worship at eleven o'clock: and we met again in the evening at six, when I married the officer of the post, and baptized his two children. On the following morning, I saw an Indian corpse staged, or put upon a few cross sticks, about ten feet from the ground, at a short distance from the fort. The property of the dead, which may consist of a kettle, axe, and a few additional articles, is generally put into the case, or wrapped in the buffaloe skin with the body, under the idea that the deceased will want them, or that the spirit of these articles will accompany the departed spirit in travelling to another world. And whenever they visit the stage or burying-place, which they frequently do for years afterwards, they will encircle it, smoke their pipes, weep bitterly, and, in their sorrow, cut themselves with knives, or pierce themselves with the points of sharp instruments. I could not but reflect that theirs is a sorrow without hope: all is *gross darkness* with them as to futurity; and they wander through life without the consolatory and cheering influence of that gospel which has brought life and immortality to light.

Before I left this post, I married two of the Company's servants, and baptized ten or twelve children. As their parents could read, I distributed some Bibles and Testaments, with some Religious Tracts among them. On the 24th, we set off for Qu'appelle, but not without the kind attention of the officer, in adding two armed servants to our party, from the expectation that we might fall in with a tribe of Stone Indians, who had been threatening him, and had acted in a turbulent manner at the post a few days before. In the course of the afternoon, we saw a band of buffaloes, which fled from us with considerable rapidity. Though an animal apparently of a very unwieldy make, and as large as a Devonshire ox, they were soon out of our sight in a laboured canter. In the evening our encampment was surrounded by wolves, which serenaded us with their melancholy howling throughout the night: and when I first put my head from under the buffaloe robe in the morning, our encampment presented a truly wild and striking scene;—the guns were resting against a tree, and pistols with powder horns were hanging on its branches; one of the men had just recruited the fire, and was cooking a small piece of buffaloe meat on the point of a stick, while the others were lying around it in every direction. Intermingled with the party were the dogs, lying in holes which they had scratched in the snow for shelter, but from which they were soon dragged, and harnessed that we might recommence our journey. We had not proceeded far before we met one of the Company's servants going to the fort which we had left, who told us that the Indians we were apprehensive of meeting had gone from their track considerably to the north of our direction. In consequence of this information we sent back the two armed servants who had accompanied us. In the course of the day we saw vast numbers of buffaloes; some rambling through the plains, while others in sheltered spots were scraping the snow away with their feet to graze. In the evening we encamped among some dwarf willows; and some time after we had kindled the fire, we were considerably alarmed by hearing the Indians drumming, shouting, and dancing, at a short distance from us in the woods. We immediately almost extinguished the fire, and lay down with our guns under our heads, fully expecting that they had seen our fire, and would visit us in the course of the night. We dreaded this from the known character of the Stone Indians, they being great thieves; and it having been represented to us, that they murdered individuals, or small parties of white people, for plunder; or stripped them, leaving them to travel to the posts without clothing, in the most severe weather. We had little sleep, and started before break of day, without having been observed by them. We stopped to breakfast at the *Standing Stone*, where the Indians had deposited bits of tobacco, small pieces of cloth, &c. as a sacrifice, in superstitious expectation that it would influence their manitou to give them buffaloes and a good hunt. Jan. 27th. soon after midnight, we were disturbed by the buffaloes passing close to our encampment: we rose early, and arrived at Qu'appelle about three o'clock. Nearly about the same time, a large band of Indians came to the fort from the plains with provisions. Many of them rode good horses, caparisoned with a saddle or pad of dressed skin, stuffed with buffaloe wool, from which were suspended wooden stirrups; and a leathern thong, tied at both ends to the under jaw of the animal, formed the bridle. When they had delivered their loads, they paraded the fort with an air of independence. It was not long however before they became clamorous for spiritous liquors; and the evening presented such a bacchanalia, including the women and the children, as I never before witnessed. Drinking made them quarrelsome, and one of the men became so infuriated, that he would have killed another with his bow, had not the master of the post immediately rushed in and taken it from him. The following day, being Sunday, the servants were all assembled for divine worship, and again in the evening. Before I left the fort, I married several of the Company's servants, who had been living with, and had families by, Indian or half-caste women, and baptized their children. I explained to them the nature and obligations of marriage and baptism; and distributed among them some Bibles and Testaments, and Religious Tracts.

With the Indians who were at the Fort, there was one of the Company's servants who had been with the tribe nearly a year and a half, to learn their language as an interpreter. They were very partial to him, and treated him with great kindness and hospitality. He usually lived with their chief, and upon informing him who I was, and the object for which I came to the country, he welcomed me by a hearty shake of the hand; while others came round me, and stroked me on the head, as a fond father would his favourite boy. On one occasion, when I particularly noticed one of their children, the boy's father was so affected with the attention, that with tears he exclaimed, ""See! the God takes notice of my child."" Many of these Indians were strong, athletic men, and generally well-proportioned; their countenances were pleasing, with aquiline noses, and beautifully white and regular teeth. The buffaloe supplies them with food, and also with clothing. The skin was the principal, and almost the only article of dress they wore, and was wrapped round them, or worn tastefully over the shoulder like the Highland plaid. The leggins of some of them were fringed with human hair, taken from the scalps of their enemies; and their moccassins, or shoes, were neatly ornamented with porcupine quills. They are notorious horse-stealers, and often make predatory excursions to the Mandan villages on the banks of the Missouri, to steal them. They sometimes visit the Red River for this purpose, and have swept off, at times, nearly the whole of our horses from the settlement. Such indeed is their propensity for this species of theft, that they have fired upon, and killed the Company's servants, close to the forts for these useful animals. They run the buffaloe with them in the summer, and fasten them to sledges which they drag over the snow when they travel in the winter; while the dogs carry burdens upon their backs, like packs upon the pack-horse. It does not appear that chastity is much regarded among them. They take as many wives as they please, and part with them for a season, or permit others to cohabit with them in their own lodges for a time, for a gun, a horse, or some article they may wish to possess. They are known, however, to kill the woman, or cut off her ears or nose, if she be unfaithful without their knowledge or permission. All the lowest and most laborious drudgery is imposed upon her, and she is not permitted to eat till after her lord has finished his meal, who amidst the burdensome toil of life, and a desultory and precarious existence, will only condescend to carry his gun, take care of his horse, and hunt as want may compel him. During the time the interpreter was with these Indians the measles prevailed, and carried off great numbers of them, in different tribes. They often expressed to him a very low opinion of the white people who introduced this disease amongst them, and threatened to kill them all, at the same time observing, that they would not hurt him, but send him home down the Missouri. When their relations, or children of whom they are passionately fond, were sick, they were almost constantly addressing their manitou drumming, and making a great noise; and at the same time they sprinkled them with water where they complained of pain. And when the interpreter was sick, they were perpetually wanting to drum and conjure him well. He spoke to them of that God and Saviour whom white people adore; but they called him a fool, saying that he never came to their country, or did any thing for them, ""*So vain were they in their imaginations, and their foolish heart was darkened.*""

Jan. 30.—We left Qu'appelle to return to the colony, and stopped for the night at an encampment of Indians, some of whom were engaged as hunters for the company. They welcomed me with much cordiality to their wigwams. We smoked the calumet as a token of friendship; and a plentiful supply of buffaloe tongues was prepared for supper. I slept in one of their tents, wrapt in a buffaloe robe, before a small fire in the centre, but the wind drawing under it, I suffered more from cold than when I slept in an open encampment. As we were starting the next morning I observed a fine looking little boy standing by the side of the cariole, and told his father that if he would send him to me at the Settlement by the first opportunity, I would be as a parent to him, clothe him, and feed him, and teach him what I knew would be for his happiness, with the Indian boys I had already under my care. We proceeded, and after we had travelled about three hours, the whole scene around us was animated with buffaloes; so numerous, that there could not be less, I apprehend, than ten thousand, in different bands, at one time in our view. It took us nearly the whole day to cross the plain, before we came to any wood for the night. We resumed our journey at the dawn of the following morning, and after travelling about three hours we stopped at a small creek to breakfast: as soon as we had kindled the fire, two Indians made their appearance, and pointing to the willows, shewed me a buffaloe that they had just shot. They were very expert in cutting up the animal, and ate some of the fat, I observed, with a few choice pieces, in a raw state. Soon afterwards I saw another Indian peeping over an eminence, whose head-dress at first gave him the appearance of a wolf: and, fearing some treachery, we hurried our breakfast and started.

Feb. 2.—The night was so intensely cold that I had but little sleep, and we hurried from our encampment at break of day. The air was filled with small icy particles; and some snow having fallen the evening before, one of the men was obliged to walk in snow shoes, to make a track for the dogs to follow. Our progress was slow, but we persevered, and arrived at Brandon house about four o'clock. We saw some persons at this post, who had just come from the Mandan villages: they informed us of the custom that prevails among these Indians, as with many others, of presenting females to strangers; the husband his wife or daughter, and the brother his sister, as a mark of hospitality: and parents are known to lend their daughters of tender age for a few beads or a little tobacco! During our stay, a Sunday intervened, when all met for divine worship in the morning and evening, and I had an opportunity of baptizing several more children, whose parents had come in from the hunting grounds, since my arrival at the Post, in my way to Qu'appelle. On the 5th we left the fort, and returning by the same track that we came, I searched for traces of my favourite lost dog, but found none. The next morning I got into the cariole very early, and the rising sun gradually opened to my view a beautiful and striking scenery. All nature appeared silently and impressively to proclaim the goodness and wisdom of God. Day unto day, in the revolutions of that glorious orb, which shed a flood of light over the impenetrable forests and wild wastes that surrounded me, uttereth speech. Yet His voice is not heard among the heathen, nor His name known throughout these vast territories by Europeans in general, but to swear by.— — Oh! for wisdom, truly Christian faith, integrity and zeal in my labours as a minister, in this heathen and *moral desert*.

Feb. 9.—The wind drifted the snow this morning like a thick fog, that at times we could scarcely see twenty yards from the cariole. It did not stop us however in our way, and I reached the farm about five o'clock, with grateful thanks to God, for protecting me through a perilous journey, drawn by dogs over the snow a distance of between five and six hundred miles among some of the most treacherous tribes of Indians in this northern wilderness.

March 4.—The weather continues very cold, so as to prevent the women and the children from attending regularly divine service on the Sabbath. The sun however is seldom obscured with clouds, but shines with a sickly face; without softening at all at present, the piercing north-westerly wind that prevails throughout the winter.

A wish having been expressed to me, that I would attend a general meeting of the principal settlers at Pembina, I set off in a cariole for this point of the Settlement, a distance of nearly eighty miles, on the 12th. We stopped a few hours at the Salt Springs, and then proceeded on our journey so as to reach Fort Daer the next morning to breakfast; so expeditiously will the dogs drag the cariole in a good track, and with a good driver. We met for the purpose of considering the best means of protection, and of resisting any attack that might be made by the Sioux Indians, who were reported to have hostile intentions against this part of the colony, in the Spring. They had frequently killed the hunters upon the plains; and a war party from the Mississippi, scalped a boy last summer within a short distance of the fort where we were assembled; leaving a painted stick upon the mangled body, as a supposed indication that they would return for slaughter.

The 18th being the Sabbath, I preached to a considerable number of persons assembled at the Fort. They heard me with great attention; but I was often depressed in mind, on the general view of character, and at the spectacle of human depravity and barbarism I was called to witness. During my stay, I went to some hunter's tents on the plains, and saw them kill the buffaloe, by crawling on the snow, and pushing their guns before them, and this for a considerable distance till they got very near the band. Their approach to the animals was like the appearance of wolves, which generally hover round them to devour the leg-wearied and the wounded; and they killed three before the herd fled. But in hunting the buffaloes for provisions it affords great diversion to pursue them on horseback. I once accompanied two expert hunters to witness this mode of killing them. It was in the spring: at this season the bulls follow the bands of cows in the rear on their return to the south, whereas in the beginning of the winter, in their migration to the north, they preceded them and led the way. We fell in with a herd of about forty, on an extensive prarie. They were covering the retreat of the cows. As soon as our horses espied them they shewed great spirit, and became as eager to chase them as I have understood the old English hunter is to follow the fox-hounds in breaking cover. The buffaloes were grazing, and did not start till we approached within about half a mile of them, when they all cantered off in nearly a compact body. We immediately threw the reins upon the horses' necks, and in a short time were intermingled with several of them. Pulling up my horse I then witnessed the interesting sight of the hunters continuing the chase, till they had separated one of the bulls from the rest, and after driving it some distance, they gallopped alongside and fired upon the animal, with the gun resting upon the front of the saddle. Immediately it was wounded, it gave chase in the most furious manner, and the horses aware of their danger, turned and cantered away at the same pace as the buffaloe. While the bull was pursuing them, the men reloaded their guns, which they do in a most expeditious manner, by pouring the charge of powder into the palm of their hand half closed, from a horn hung over the shoulder, and taking a ball from the pouch that is fastened to their side, and then suddenly breaking out of the line, they shot the animal through the heart as it came opposite to them. It was of a very large size, with long shaggy hair on the head and shoulders, and the head when separated from the carcase was nearly as much as I could lift from the ground.

The Indians have another mode of pursuing the buffaloes for subsistence, by driving them into a pound. They make the inclosure of a circular form with trees felled on the spot, to the extent of one or two hundred yards in diameter, and raise the entrance with snow, so as to prevent the retreat of the animals when they have once entered. As soon as a herd is seen in the horizon coming in the direction of the pound, a party of Indians arrange themselves singly in two opposite lines, branching out gradually on each side to a considerable distance, that the buffaloes may advance between them. In taking their station at the distance of twenty or thirty yards from each other, they lie down, while another party manœuvre on horseback, to get in rear of the band. Immediately they have succeeded they give chace, and the party in ambush rising up as the buffaloes come opposite to them, they all halloo, and shout, and fire their guns, so as to drive them, trampling upon each other, into the snare, where they are soon slaughtered by the arrow or the gun.

The buffaloe tongue, when well cured, is of excellent flavour, and is much esteemed, together with the *bos*, or hump of the animal, that is formed on the point of the shoulders. The meat is much easier of digestion than English beef; and many pounds of it are often taken by the hungry traveller just before he wraps himself in his buffaloe robe for the night without the least inconvenience.

On my return to the Fort, I had an opportunity of hearing from a chief of a small tribe of Chipewyans, surrounded by a party of his young men, a most pathetic account, and a powerful declaration of revenge against the Sioux Indians, who had tomahawked and scalped his son. Laying his hand upon his heart as he related the tragical circumstance, he emphatically exclaimed, 'It is *here* I am affected, and *feel* my loss;' then raising his hand above his head, he said, 'the spirit of my son cries for vengeance. It must be appeased. His bones lie on the ground uncovered. We want ammunition: give us powder and ball, and we will go and revenge his death upon our enemies.' Their public speeches are full of bold metaphor, energy and pathos. ""No Greek or Roman orator ever spoke perhaps with more strength and sublimity than one of their chiefs when asked to remove with his tribe to a distance from their native soil."" 'We were born,' said he, 'on this ground, our fathers lie buried in it, shall we say to the bones of our fathers, arise, and come with us into a foreign land?'

One of the Indians left his wampum, or belt, at the Fort as a pledge that he would return and pay the value of an article which was given to him at his request. They consider this deposit sacred and inviolable, and as giving a sanction to their words, their promises and their treaties. They are seldom known to fail in redeeming the pledge; and they ratify their agreements with each other by a mutual exchange of the wampum, regarding it with the smoking of tobacco, as the great test of sincerity.

In conducting their war excursions, they act upon the same principle as in hunting. They are vigilant in espying out the track of those whom they pursue, and will follow them over the praries, and through the forests, till they have discovered where they halt; when they wait with the greatest patience, under every privation, either lurking in the grass, or concealing themselves in the bushes, till an opportunity offers to rush upon their prey, at a time when they are least able to resist them. These tribes are strangers to open warfare, and laugh at Europeans as fools for standing out, as they say, in the plains, to be shot at.

On the 22nd I reached the Farm, and from the expeditious mode of travelling over the snow, I began to think, as is common among the Indians, that one hundred miles was little more than a step, or in fact but a short distance. It often astonished me to see with what an unwearied pace, the drivers hurry along their dogs in a cariole, or sledge, day after day in a journey of two and three hundred miles. I have seen some of the English half-breeds greatly excel in this respect. Many of the Canadians however are very expert drivers, as they are excellent *voyageurs* in the canoe. There is a native gaiety, and vivacity of character, which impel them forward, and particularly so, under the individual and encouraging appellation of '*bon homme*.' When tripping, they are commonly all life, using the whip, or more commonly a thick stick, barbarously upon their dogs, vociferating as they go ""*Sacres Crapeaux,*"" ""*Sacrée Marne,*"" ""*Saintes Diables,*"" and uttering expressions of the most appalling blasphemy. In the rivers, their canoe songs, as sung to a lively air and chorus with the paddle, are very cheerful and pleasing. They smoke immediately and almost incessantly, when the paddle is from their hands; and none exceed them in skill, in running the rapids, passing the portages with pieces of eighty and ninety pounds weight upon their backs, and expeditiously performing a journey of one thousand miles.

April 1.—Last Friday I married several couples, at the Company's Post; nearly all the English half-breeds were assembled on the occasion, and so passionately fond are they of dancing, that they continued to dance almost incessantly from two o'clock on Friday afternoon, till late on Saturday night. This morning the Colony Fort was nearly thronged with them to attend divine service; and it was my endeavour to address them, with plainness, simplicity, and fidelity. There was much attention; but, I fear, from their talking, principally, their mother tongue, the Indian language, that they did not comprehend a great deal of my discourse. This is the case also, with a few of the Scotch Highland settlers, who speak generally the Gaelic language.

Marriage, I would enforce upon all, who are living with, and have children by half-caste, or Indian women. The apostolic injunction is clear and decisive against the too common practice of the country, in putting them away, after enjoying the morning of their days; or deserting them to be taken by the Indians with their children, when the parties, who have cohabited with them, leave the Hudson's Bay Company's territories.[2] And if a colony is to be organized, and established in the wilderness, the moral obligation of marriage must be felt. It is ""the *parent*,"" said Sir William Scott, ""not the *child* of civil society."" Some *form*, or religious rite in marriage is also requisite, and has generally been observed by enlightened and civilized nations. It is a civil contract in civil society, but the sanction of religion should be superadded. The ancients considered it as a religious ceremony. They consulted their imaginary gods, before the marriage was solemnized, and implored their assistance by prayers, and sacrifices; the gall was taken out of the victim, as the seat of anger and malice, and thrown behind the altar, as hateful to the deities who presided over the nuptial ceremonies. Marriage, by its original institution[3] is the nearest of all earthly relations, and as involving each other's happiness through life, it surely ought to be entered upon by professing Christians, with religious rites, invoking heaven as a party to it, while the consent of the individuals is pledged to each other, ratified and confirmed by a vow.

Incestuous cohabitation is common with the Indians, and in some instances, they will espouse several sisters at the same time; but so far from adopting the custom of others in presenting their wives, or daughters as a mark of hospitality due to a stranger, the Chipewyans or Saulteaux tribe of Red River, appear very jealous of them towards Europeans. There is something patriarchal in their manner of first choosing their wives. When a young man wishes to take a young woman to live with him; he may perhaps mention his wishes to her, but generally, he speaks to the father, or those who have authority over her. If his proposal be accepted, he is admitted into the tent, and lives with the family, generally a year, bringing in the produce of his hunting for the general mess. He then separates to a tent of his own, and adds to the number of wives, according to his success and character as a hunter. The Indians have been greatly corrupted in their simple and barbarous manners, by their intercourse with Europeans, many of whom have borne scarcely any other mark of the Christian character than the name; and who have not only fallen into the habits of an Indian life, but have frequently exceeded the savage in their savage customs. When a female is taken by them, it does not appear that her wishes are at all consulted, but she is obtained from the lodge as an inmate at the Fort, for the prime of her days generally, through that irresistible bribe to Indians, rum. Childbirth, is considered by them, as an event of a trifling nature; and it is not an uncommon case for a woman to be taken in labour, step aside from the party she is travelling with, and overtake them in the evening at their encampment, with a new-born infant on her back. It has been confidently stated that Indian women suffer more from parturition with half-breed children than when the father is an Indian. If this account be true, it can only be in consequence of their approach to the habits of civilized life, exerting an injurious influence over their general constitution. When taken to live with white men, they have larger families, and at the same time are liable to more disease consequent upon it, than in their wild and wandering state. They have customs, such as separation for forty days at the birth of a child, setting apart the female in a separate lodge at peculiar seasons, and forbidding her to touch any articles in common use, which bear a strong resemblance to the laws of uncleanness, and separation commanded to be observed towards Jewish females. These strongly corroborate the idea, that they are of Asiatic origin; descended from some of the scattered tribes of the children of Israel: and through some ancient transmigration, came over by Kamtchatka into these wild and extensive territories. When they name their children, it is common for them to make a feast, smoke the calumet, and address the Master of life, asking him to protect the child, whom they call after some animal, place, or object in nature, and make him a good hunter. The Stone Indians add to the request, a good horse-stealer. The women suckle their children generally, till the one supplants the other, and it is not an uncommon circumstance to see them of three or four years old running to take the breast. They have a burial ground at the Settlement, and usually put the property of the deceased into the grave with the corpse. If any remains, it is given away from an aversion they have to use any thing that belonged to their relations who have died. Some of the graves are very neatly covered over with short sticks and bark as a kind of canopy, and a few scalps are affixed to poles that are stuck in the ground at the head of several of them. You see also occasionally at the grave, a piece of wood on which is either carved or painted the symbols of the tribe the deceased belonged to, and which are taken from the different animals of the country.

April 6.—One of the principal settlers informed me this morning, that an Indian had stabbed one of his wives in a fit of intoxication at an encampment near his house. I immediately went to the Lodge to inquire into the circumstance, and found that the poor woman had been stabbed in wanton cruelty, through the shoulder and the arm, but not mortally. The Indians were still drunk, and some of them having knives in their hands, I thought it most prudent to withdraw from their tents, without offering any assistance. The Indians appear to me to be generally of an inoffensive and hospitable disposition; but spirituous liquors, like war, infuriate them with the most revengeful and barbarous feelings. They are so conscious of this effect of drinking, that they generally deliver up their guns, bows and arrows, and knives, to the officers, before they begin to drink at the Company's Post; and when at their tents, it is the first care of the women to conceal them, during the season of riot and intoxication.

A considerable quantity of snow fell on the night of the 12th, and the weather continuing very cold, it is not practicable yet to begin any operations in farming. Though I see not as yet any striking effects of my ministry among the settlers, yet, I trust, some little outward reformation has taken place, in the better observance of the Sabbath.

May 2.—The rivers have broken up this spring unusually late, and the ice is now floating down in large masses. The settlers, who went to Pembina and the plains, for buffaloe meat in the Fall, are returning upon rafts, or in canoes formed by hollowing the large trunks of trees: many of them are as improvident of to-morrow as the Indians, and have brought with them no dried provisions for the summer. This is not the case however with the Scotch, who have been provident enough to bring with them a supply of dried meat and pemican for a future day. The dried meat is prepared by cutting the flesh of the buffaloe thin, and hanging it on stages of wood to dry by the fire; and is generally tied in bundles of fifty or forty pounds weight. It is very rough, and tasteless, except a strong flavour of the smoke. Pemican is made by pounding the dried meat, and mixing it with boiled fat, and is then put into bags made of buffaloe skin, which weigh about eighty and a hundred pounds each. It is a species of food well adapted to travelling in the country; but so strongly cemented in the bag, that when it is used, it is necessary to apply the axe; and very much resembles in appearance tallow-chandler's grease.

The 10th.—The plains have been on fire to a considerable extent for several days past, and the awful spectacle is seen this evening, through the whole of the northern, and western horizon. Idle rumours prevail that the Sioux Indians will attack the Settlement; which unhappily unsettle the minds, and interrupt the industry of the colonists. But none of these things move me, in carrying on my plans, and making arrangements to erect a substantial building, sixty feet by twenty. The Red River appears to me, a most desirable spot for a Missionary establishment, and the formation of schools; from whence Christianity may arise, and be propagated among the numerous tribes of the north. The settlers are now actively employed in preparing to sow the small lots of land which they have cleared: but this season is short from the great length of the winter.—The 20th being Sunday more than one hundred of them assembled at the Fort for divine service; and their children from the school were present for public examination. They gave general satisfaction in their answers to questions from the ""Chief Truths of the Christian Religion, and Lewis's Catechism.""—Text Proverbs iii. 17.

By the arrival of the boats from Qu'appelle, on the 25th, I received the little Indian boy, I noticed, when leaving the Hunter's Tents, during my excursion to that quarter in January last. Soon after my departure, the father of the boy observed, that ""as I had asked for his son, and stood between the Great Spirit and the Indians, he would send him to me;"" and just before the boats left the Post for the Red River, he brought the boy, and requested that he might be delivered to my care. Thus was I encouraged in the idea, that native Indian children might be collected from the wandering tribes of the north, and educated in ""the knowledge of the true God, and Jesus Christ whom he hath sent.""

Every additional Indian child I obtained for this purpose, together with the great inconvenience of having no place appropriated for public worship, gave a fresh stimulus to exertion in erecting the proposed building. There was but little willing assistance however, towards this desirable object; as few possessed any active spirit of public improvement; and the general habits of the people being those of lounging and smoking, were but little favourable to voluntary exertions.

Sturgeon are caught at this period, from sixty to one hundred pounds weight and more, in great abundance at the Settlement; and also for about a month in the fall of the year, a little below the rapids towards the mouth of the river. The oil of this fish is sometimes used as lamp oil by the settlers; and the sound, when carefully and quickly dried in the shade, by hanging it upon a line in a good breeze, forms isinglass, the simple solution of which in water makes a good jelly, and may be seasoned by the addition of syrup and wine, or of the expressed juices of any ripe fruit. The roe is often cooked immediately it is taken from the fish; but, when salted and placed under a considerable pressure until dry, it forms the very nutritious article of food named *caviare*. They generally afford us an abundant supply of provisions for about a month or five weeks; and when they leave the river, we have usually a good supply of cat fish, weighing about seven or eight pounds each, and which are taken in greater or less quantities for the most part of the summer months.

June the 20th. The canoes arrived from Montreal, *via* Lake Superior, and brought me the gratifying intelligence, in letters from England, that my family were all well. It was my intention that they should have embarked with me in my mission to this country, but circumstances prevented it; and now that I was surrounded with unexpected difficulties, situated in the very heart of an Indian territory, most difficult of access, and without military protection, I deemed it most advisable that they should defer the voyage, in the hope that another year might lessen these difficulties, and bring a better arrangement for the prosperity of the colony. I could undergo privations, and enter upon any arduous official duties, for the best interests of the natives and the settlers; but I could not subject Mrs. West (and infant children) to the known existing trials of the country, whose useful talents would otherwise have greatly aided me in the formation and superintendence of schools.

July 2nd. An agreeable change has taken place in the scenery around us; the trees are breaking into leaves, and many plants are in blossom, where, but a short time ago, everything bore the aspect of winter. But this almost sudden and pleasing change has brought an unceasing torment: night and day we are perpetually persecuted with the mosquitoes, that swarm around us, and afford no rest but in the annoying respiration of a smoky room. They hover in clouds about the domestic cattle, and drive them (almost irritated to madness) to the smoke of fires lighted with tufts of grass for their relief. The trial of this ever busy and tormenting insect is inconceivable, but to those who have endured it. We retire to rest, enveloped in clothes almost to suffocation, but the musquitoe finds its way under the blankets, piercing with its envenomed trunk, till we often rise in a fever. Nor are we relieved from this painful scourge until the return of a slight frost, in the beginning of September.

20th. The weather is extremely hot, the thermometer more than 90°#176; above zero. Vegetation is making an astonishingly rapid progress, and the grain in its luxuriant growth upon a rich soil, presents to the eye the fairest prospects of a good harvest. But the locust, an insect very like the large grasshopper, is beginning to make sad ravages, by destroying the crops, as it has done for the last three years, at the Settlement. These insects multiply so rapidly, that they soon overspread the land, or rather the whole country; and had not a wise Providence limited their existence to a year, they would no doubt (if permitted to increase) soon destroy the whole vegetative produce of the world. They seem to devour, not so much from a ravenous appetite, as from the rage of destroying every vegetable substance that lies in the way; and their work of destruction is frequently so regular in a field of corn, as to have the appearance of being cut with a scythe. Where they are bred, from eggs that are deposited in the earth the autumn before, they stop during the months of April, May, and June; towards the latter end of July, they get strong, and have wings, when they rise together, sometimes so numerous as to form a black cloud, which darkens the rays of the sun. Their first direction is against the wind, but afterwards they appear to be driven by its course, and fall, as a scourge, as they become exhausted by flight. ""*The land may be as the garden of Eden before them, but behind them it is a desolate wilderness.*""

CHAPTER III.

NORWAY HOUSE. BAPTISMS. ARRIVAL AT YORK FACTORY. SWISS EMIGRANTS. AUXILIARY BIBLE SOCIETY FORMED. BOAT WRECKED. CATHOLIC PRIESTS. SIOUX INDIANS KILLED AT THE COLONY. CIRCULATION OF THE SCRIPTURES AMONG THE COLONISTS. SCARCITY OF PROVISIONS. FISHING UNDER THE ICE. WILD FOWL. MEET THE INDIANS AT PEMBINA. THEY SCALP AN ASSINIBOINE. WAR DANCE. CRUELLY PUT TO DEATH A CAPTIVE BOY. INDIAN EXPRESSION OF GRATITUDE FOR THE EDUCATION OF HIS CHILD. STURGEON.

The late Earl of Selkirk having suggested that, ""In the course of each summer, it would be proper that the minister should visit the Hudson's Bay Company's factory at Norway House, and also at York Fort, as a great number of their servants are assembled at these places, for a few weeks in summer, and have no other opportunity for any public religious instruction;"" I left the settlement on the first of August, and met, at Norway House, one of the Directors of the Hudson's Bay Company, and a gentleman of the North West, on their route from Montreal to York Fort, to make arrangements for the future trade of the country, in consequence of a coalition between the two Companies. This was a circumstance which I could not but hail, as highly encouraging in the attempt to better the condition of the native Indians, and likely to remove many of the evils that prevailed during the ardour of opposition.

The 12th of August, being Sunday, we had divine service; after which I baptized between twenty and thirty children, and married two of the Company's officers. On the 14th, we left this Post, and arrived at York Factory, the 27th, where we found a considerable number of Swiss families, who had left their country, as emigrants to the Red River Colony. They shewed me a prospectus, which had been circulated in the Swiss Cantons, by a gentleman who had been in Canada, but had never seen the Settlement; and were anxious in their inquiries whether it was rising to prosperity. They appeared to me to be a different description of settlers, from what the colony, in its infancy of improvement, was prepared to receive; as consisting principally of watchmakers and mechanics. The hardy husbandman was the character we wanted; who would work his persevering way through the thickets, clear the surface, and spread cultivation around us; and not easily repine if a storm overtook him in the wilderness.

During my stay at the Factory, several marriages and baptisms took place; and it was no small encouragement to me, in my ministerial labours, to have the patronage and cordial co-operation of the Director I had the pleasure of meeting, in establishing an Auxiliary Bible Society, for ""Prince Rupert's Land and the Red River Settlement."" It was formed with great liberality on the part of the Company's officers, who met on the occasion; and more than one hundred and twenty pounds were immediately subscribed, in aid of an institution, (the British and Foreign Bible Society,) which justly challenges the admiration of the world. Pure in its principle, and simple yet mighty in operation, it is diffusing blessings through the four quarters of the globe: Europe, Asia, Africa, and America, are partakers of its bounty; and the tide of its beneficent liberality is flowing towards all nations, kindreds, tongues, and complexions of our fellow men, that they may read in their own tongues the wonderful works of God.

We cheered the Director, with the most cordial feelings of regard, as he stepped into the boat, on the morning of the 13th of September, to embark in the Prince of Wales, on his return to England; and immediately afterwards, I set off on my return to the Red River. We overtook the second division of boats, with the Swiss emigrants, on the 20th, slowly proceeding, and greatly harassed with the difficulties of the navigation. They informed us, that one of their party was accidentally drowned, soon after they left the Factory; and that several of their children had died on the passage. We were late on our return to the colony, and under considerable apprehensions that the rivers would be frozen over before our arrival. We experienced very cold weather the beginning of October; and our encampment at night was frequently covered with snow. One of the Swiss got his feet dreadfully frozen, from the careless neglect of not taking off his shoes and socks to dry, before he lay down to rest. In crossing Winipeg Lake, one of the boats was wrecked, but providentially no lives were lost. This accident, however, detained us in an encampment for six or seven days; and having scarcely any other subsistence than a little boiled barley, I experienced at times the most pressing hunger. Every one rambled in pursuit of game, but generally returned unsuccessful. One evening, a servant brought in from his day's hunt a large horned owl, which was immediately cooked, and eagerly despatched. The next day, I was walking along the shore with my gun, when the waves cast at my feet a dead jack-fish; I took it up, and felt, from the keenness of my appetite for animal food, as though I could have immediately devoured it, notwithstanding it bore the marks of having been dead a considerable time. At this moment, I heard the croaking of a raven, and placing the fish upon the bank, as a bait, I shot it from behind a willow, where I had concealed myself, as it lighted upon the ground; and the success afforded me a welcome repast at night.

We reached the mouth of the Red River on the 2nd of November, and found our friend Pigewis, the Indian chief, at his old encampment. He received us most hospitably, giving us a good supply of dried sturgeon. Our hungry party put the liberality of the Indians to the test, but it did not fail; as I believe it seldom does, in their improvidence of tomorrow. I landed at Fort Douglas on the 4th, and could not but recount the mercies of God in my safe return. They have followed me through many a perilous, and trying scene of life; and I would that a sense of a continual protecting Providence in the mercy of Redemption, may ever actuate me in whatsoever things may tend to the promotion of the happiness, and of the *best interests* of my fellow men, in the journeyings of my life, through a disordered and distracted world.

No sooner had the Swiss emigrants arrived, than many of the Germans, who had come to the Settlement a few years ago from Canada, and had houses, presented themselves 'in search of a wife,' and having fixed their attachment with acceptance, they received those families, in which was their choice, into their habitations. Those who had no daughters to afford this introduction, were obliged to pitch their tents along the banks of the river, and outside the stockades of the Fort, till they removed to Pembina in the better prospect of provisions for the winter. Those of the Germans, who were Catholics, applied to the Canadian Catholic Priests to solemnize their marriage; but they refused, because their intended wives were Protestants; and such was their bigotry in this matter, in refusing to marry a Catholic to a Protestant, that they expressed an opinion, that a Catholic could not be present, even as a witness, ""*sine culpa*""[4] when I performed the marriage ceremony, ""*inter Catholicos et Hæreticos*.""[5]

The locusts which had begun the work of destruction at my leaving the Colony for York Factory, had completely destroyed the crops; and during my absence, a party of Sioux Indians, came to Fort Douglas, in expectation, it was said, of receiving presents from the stores. It was thought advisable to promise them some goods, on their returning peaceably to their own country, and they manifested no other than a peaceable disposition to all parties. The Saulteaux Indians, however, of Red River, between whom and the Sioux nation, a hostile feeling has existed from time immemorial, became very irritable; and a small party of them fired upon a straggling party of the Sioux, in a garden on the Point below the Colony Fort; they killed two, and wounded a third; and fled with such precipitation by swimming the river, and running through the willows, as to escape the vengeance, and almost the view of those who survived. It is the glory of the North American Indian to steal upon his enemies like a fox, to attack like a tiger, and flee after the attack like a bird. The Indians were not seen any more till after the Sioux had left the settlement, who went away murmuring, that powder and ball had been given, as they said, at the Fort, to the Saulteaux, to kill them. In fact they had formed a deep laid scheme to scalp the person in charge of Fort Douglas, in the absence of the 'Chargè d'Affaires' of the Colony, and were only prevented carrying it into execution by one of the party giving information to a person at the Farm, as to their intentions. They buried those who were shot near the Stockades of the Fort, and for more than a week after they were gone, the Saulteaux, in their savage fondness to exhibit the scalp in their war-dance, and obtain possession of the toes and fingers of the slain, made several attempts by night to disturb the graves, but were prevented getting these trophies, by a watch that was kept.

November 11.—The winter is again set in with severity, and I have been greatly disappointed in not having the building so far finished, as to have accommodated the schoolmaster with a residence, as well as to have afforded a place for divine worship before this period. He is now resident with the Indian boys, at the Post which formerly belonged to the North West Company: but being so far distant from the body of the Protestant settlers his number of scholars is not so large as it was, nor have we so many on the Sabbath, for divine worship as formerly. The difficulties which we have hitherto met with in obtaining provisions, and the mode of procuring them, have formed the character of the Colonists principally into that of hunters and fishermen; so that labourers are not obtained but at a high remunerating price, or at a dollar a day each. A circulating medium would no doubt reduce the price of labour. It has frequently been requested by the settlers, and would relieve them from many unpleasant circumstances arising from barter and payment by bills.

I found the Scriptures at some of the Company's Posts I visited, most of the copies of which had been sent into the country, together with the Book of Common Prayer, by one of the Directors, who ever expressed to me a lively interest for its moral improvement: and the liberal supply which I had received from the British and Foreign Bible Society, in several different languages, enabled me to circulate many copies of the Bible among the colonists, in *English, Gaelic, German, Danish, Italian,* and *French.* They were gratefully received by them in general, and by none more so than the Highlanders, one of whom on receiving a Gaelic Bible well remarked, ""that one word in the heart was worth more than the whole volume in the pocket neglected."" The Catholic priests, however, opposed this circulation, and one of them called on a Catholic, to whom I had given a Bible at his own particular request, and after anathematizing our great reformer, asked him to give it up. The man refused with this pointed and pertinent question, ""From whence, Sir, do you get your knowledge of religion?"" In this refusal, he acted upon the enlightened principle, that we derive all true sentiments in religious subjects from the Bible, and the Bible alone; and that the exercise of private judgment in the possession of the Bible, was the birth-right privilege of every man. Therein is contained the great charter of salvation, and the awful code of divine communication to the human race. ""A Bible then to every man in the world,"" is the sentiment we would encourage, in opposition to such a priestly objection, that is contrary to the liberal conduct of more enlightened Catholics, and manifestly opposed to scriptural examples, and the divine command of the Founder of Christianity himself. The Eunuch was *reading the scriptures*, searching for, and inquiring after divine truth, when Philip received a commission from heaven to ""join himself to his chariot."" The Saviour gave an authoritative command to the Jews to ""*search the scriptures*,"" and it is recorded of Timothy that ""*from a child he had known the Holy Scriptures*."" They are the means of affording that instruction which man's wisdom cannot teach, while they bear every mark of a divine revelation, in a manner worthy of God, and plain to the meanest capacity.

I had given a French Testament to one of the Canadians, whom I married to a Swiss Protestant, which excited the farther active prejudice of the Catholic priest. He called on him, and requested that he might have it, but the Canadian objected, saying, that as his wife was a Protestant, she wished to read it. He then asked to borrow it, promising to return the Testament in a few days, and took it home with him. I had written on the inside of the cover—

The man's name.
From the British and Foreign Bible Society.
""Sondez les Ecritures."" St. Jean, v. 39.

A short time after it was returned, the Canadian shewed me the remarks which the priest had written, and gave me the Testament, at my request, in exchange for a Bible.

Over the above text, the Catholic priest wrote, ""Lisez avee soin les Ecritures, mais ne les explicuez point d'apres vos lumieres,"" and immediately following my name, which I had put at the bottom of the cover: ""Si *quelquun* nécoute pas l'Eglise regardez le comme un Paién, et un Publicain."" Matth. xviii. 17; adding the following observations: ""Dans ce livre, on ne dit pas un mot de la penitence qui afflige le corps. Cependant il est de foi qu'elle est absolument necessaire au salut aprés le péché, c'est a l'Eglise de J. C. qu'il appartient de determiner le sens des Ecritures.""

The prejudices which the Canadian priests at the Colony express against Catholics marrying Protestants must tend to weaken the religious and moral obligation of the marriage contract, as entered into between them. I have known the priests refuse to marry the parties of the above different persuasions, at the time that they were co-habiting together, as though it were better for them to live in fornication, than that they should violate the rigid statutes of the Papal see.

I married a couple a short time ago, and afterwards found that the priest had been unwearied in calling upon the woman who was a professed Protestant, and never ceased to repeat to her their opinions of heretics, till, with the persuasion of her husband, they prevailed upon her to be re-baptized, and re-married by them in the *nominal* profession of the Catholic faith. And I was assured by a Swiss gentleman at the Settlement, who had married a Catholic from Montreal, that some months after their marriage, one of the priests called upon his wife, and told her that it would have been better for her to have married a heathen, than a Protestant. A heathen, he said, might be converted to the Catholic faith, and be saved, but little hope could be entertained of a Protestant. These circumstances prove that Popery, as it now exists, at least in this quarter of the globe, is not contrary to what it was in the days of the Reformation.

Christmas is again returned, and appears to be generally known amongst us, as in Europe, only as a season of intoxication. Will not the very heathen rise up in judgment, at the last day, and condemn such a gross perversion of the supposed period of the Redeemer's birth; the knowledge of whose name, they have hitherto been unacquainted with. We had divine service at the Fort:—text, Luke ii. 8-11. The Indian boys repeated some hymns, and joined in the singing Hallelujah! to the ""Emmanuel, which being interpreted, is, God with us."" I meet with many discouraging circumstances in my ministerial labours; but my path is sometimes cheered with the pleasing hope, that they are not altogether in vain; and that the light of Christianity will break in upon the heathen darkness that surrounds me. *The promises of God are sure*; and when cast down, I am not disheartened.

January 1, 1822.—Oh thou God of mercy, as thou hast brought me hitherto, be pleased to support and direct me in the wilderness; order my footsteps, and make my path acceptable to thyself—""Hoping all things, may I endure all things,"" in the desire of usefulness, as I proceed in the journey of life, and be endued with a

Spirit of Love, and of a sound mind, as year after year revolves over my head.

The 16th. We are suffering great privations at the Settlement. Very little buffaloe meat has been obtained from the plains, and our principal subsistence is from grain boiled into soup. Few have either pepper, salt, flour, or vegetables. One of the Swiss was lately frozen to death on the plains; and a Meuron settler returning to the colony with a horse sledge of provisions perished also from the severity of the winter.

Feb. 14.—Times do not yet wear a more favourable aspect, and most of the settlers are upon an allowance of a pint of wheat each a day. Sometimes a few fish are taken with nets, from under the ice, which are put down by making holes at the distance of about fifteen or twenty feet from each other, and affixing the net line to a pole of this length, by which the net is drawn in the water from one opening to the other, till it is easily set. The fish that are caught, are pike, perch, and a species of herring, called gold-eyes, and for which an exorbitant price is frequently paid. The northern Indians angle for fish in winter, by cutting round holes in the ice about a foot or two in diameter, and letting down a baited hook. This is always kept in motion to prevent the water from freezing, and to attract the fish to the spot. Immediately they take a fish, they scoop out the eyes and swallow them, thinking them as great a delicacy as the European does the oyster.

My professional duties calling me to Pembina, I left the Farm in a cariole on the 20th, and was sorry to find on my arrival many Swiss families suffering from the want of a regular supply of provisions from the plains. This was occasioned in a great measure from the irregularity and eagerness with which the hunters pursued the buffaloes immediately they made their appearance. Had they suffered some of the leading bands to have passed in the direction they were going towards the Settlement, instead of pursuing and turning them as soon as they were seen in the horizon, others would probably have followed, and plenty of provisions had been obtained. But the fugitive supplies of the chase are generally a poor dependance; and the colony will be greatly encouraged should the domestic cattle that have been purchased arrive from the United States. The difficulties which the Swiss emigrants have had to encounter, and the severity of the climate have disheartened many of them from settling in the country, and they have determined on going to a settlement on the Ohio in the Spring. They attended divine service on the Sabbath during my stay, and expressed much gratitude for my reading to them the French Testament and the ministerial duties I performed among them.

I returned to the Farm, where a report reached me, which was in circulation, upon strong grounds of suspicion, that a most deliberate and barbarous murder had been committed by one of the half-breeds on a Canadian freeman. He was supposed to have been instigated to the bloody deed by a woman he lived with, and whom he received from the Canadian for so many buffaloes as provision. Evidence however was wanting, it was thought, that would justify his being sent down to Montreal, or to England for trial, to convict him there; as there was no criminal jurisdiction established within the territories of the Hudson's Bay Company.

March 25.—The thaw has come on unexpectedly early, and caused many of the hunters to return from the plains with scarcely any provisions. There were a few tame buffaloes that had been reared in the colony, which have been slaughtered, and to save as much seed corn as possible, the allowance of grain is given out to the settlers with the most rigid economy by the Chargè d'Affaires. There was a general shout to day in the Settlement at the sight of some swans and geese, as the sure harbingers of Spring, and of immense flocks of wild fowl, that bend their course in the Spring to the north, as in the fall of the year they fly to the south. It was indeed a cheerful sight, as nearly all the feathered tribe leave us during a long and severe winter. In this season, we hear only, and that but very seldom the croaking of the raven, the chattering of the magpie, or the tapping of the woodpecker. But as summer bursts upon us, the call of the whip-poor-will is heard in the dusk of the evening, and the solitude of the woods is enlivened with a rich variety of birds, some of which dazzle the eye with the beauty of their colours. They have no notes however in their gay plumage, or melody of sound, which catch, and delight the ear. The wild fowl are mere birds of passage at the Red River, and but few were shot, as they passed over the colony, for our relief, in the want of provisions.

Our numbers increased almost daily, from the return of the settlers from the plains, and it was the general opinion that it would be far better to kill all the horses and dogs in the Settlement for food, than distribute the whole of the grain, so as to be without seed corn.

April 5.—One of the chief officers of the Hudson's Bay Company arrived, and gave us the welcome promise, (before we were actually driven to the above extremity,) that the Colony should receive some wheat to sow from the Company's Post at *Bas la Rivière*, on Lake Winepeg, where there is a good farm, and the crops had escaped the ravages of the locusts. When cheered by this prospect, the information reached us, that a party of Sioux Indians were on their way to the Settlement. As their intentions in visiting us were not known, and being apprehensive that more blood would be shed by the Saulteaux if they came down to Fort Douglas, it was resolved that two boats should be manned to prevent if possible their proceeding any farther than Pembina. It was far better to present an imposing force to them on the borders of the colony, than to suffer them to come down amongst us, where we should have been completely in their power, in our scattered habitations. At the request of the chief officer I accompanied the boats, and set off with him for the Company's Post at Pembina, about the middle of May. We arrived on the Friday, and soon after divine service on the Sunday morning the Sioux Indians were seen marching over the plains, with several colours flying, towards the Colony Fort, which was immediately opposite to that of the Company. When at the distance of about five hundred yards from us, they halted, and a Saulteaux Indian who happened to be at Pembina, immediately stripped himself naked, and rushed towards them as a proof of his courage. They received him with a cold reserve, while some of them pointed their guns close to his body. He then mingled with the party, and we conducted them to the Colony Fort, as is customary when Indians are supposed to visit with peaceable and friendly intentions.

As soon as they had entered the Fort they placed two sentinels at the gate, one with a bow and arrows, and the other with a gun. There was something like military discipline among them, which they had probably learned during the late American war, in which they were engaged by the English; many of them were of a remarkably fine stature, and well-proportioned, but more formed for agility than strength. Their countenances were stamped with a fierce and barbarous expression, and being all armed with either long knives, tomahawks, guns, or bows, they soon encircled and formed a guard for the Chief of their party. After a short time, they became very restless, and searched every corner and outhouse of the Fort, under the suspicion that some treacherous attack might be made upon them. A few of them then crossed over to the Company's Post, and no idea was entertained but that they would conduct themselves peaceably. Liquor was given them at both posts; and as I was standing within the stockades of that of the Company, at eight o'clock in the evening, a Chief of the party named Wanatou, came in apparently intoxicated, and snatching a gun from an Indian who stood near him, he fired it with ball in a manner that indicated some evil design. Leaving the Fort he wrestled with another for his gun which he fired in the air, and went immediately to the other post, where it was supposed they had taken up their quarters for the night. A guard being mounted, we retired to rest, but were disturbed about eleven o'clock with the cry, that the Sioux Indians had shot and scalped an Assiniboine, who with two others had travelled a considerable distance to smoke the calumet with them at Pembina. The bloody and unsuspected deed was committed by Wanatou, whose intention was to have killed the other two had they not immediately fled, because some one, or a party of their nation had stolen a horse from him about a year before. As soon as the scalp was taken they all started for the plains with this notorious Chief, who had shed the blood of ten or twelve Indians and Americans before; and who bore the marks of having been several times pierced with balls by his enemies. It was formerly the custom to cut off the heads of those whom they slew in war, and to carry them away as trophies; but these were found cumbersome in the hasty retreat which they always make as soon as they have killed their enemy; they are now satisfied with only tearing off the scalp. This is usually taken from the crown of the head, of a small circular size; sometimes however they take the whole integuments of the skull, with which they ornament their war jackets and leggins, or twist into a brush for the purpose of keeping off the mosquitoes. The scalp is their glory and triumph, and is often carried by women stretched upon a stick, and hung with various articles so as to make a jingle to men when they perform the war-dance.

This is very animated and striking, as they generally dance completely armed, and with gestures to represent their mode of going to war, their attack upon their enemy, the scalping of those who are slain, and their triumphant return as conquerors. They go through these evolutions in such a wild and savage manner as frequently to excite the fears of the European, who witnesses the war dance, lest it should terminate, in a bloody conflict, and the death of most of the party.

We returned to the Forks, after having seen a party of half-breeds set off with their horses and carts for buffaloe meat, in the same direction the Sioux Indians were gone. They were advised not to follow their track so immediately; but the want of provisions led them to neglect this advice; and in about a fortnight afterwards we were informed, that they had been fired upon in their encampment in the dawn of the morning (the time when Indians generally make their attack) that two of them were killed, a third mortally wounded, and that all their horses were stolen. It was strongly suspected though never ascertained as a fact, that this savage deed was committed by the Indians who had so recently left Pembina; as well as the scalping of one of the Company's servants who was killed a short time afterwards within a mile of the Fort.

The Sioux are a great nation, spread over a vast tract of country, between the Missisippi and Pembina; along the banks of the Missouri, and towards the Saskashawan. They are divided into numerous tribes, called Sisatoones, Yanktoons, Wapatoones, and others, with the Assiniboines or Stone Indians, who are recognized as descendents or seceders, by a similarity of language and customs. On the banks of the Mississippi and Missouri rivers they have small villages, where they grow Indian corn, pumpkins, and water melons; but they live principally on the plains in the chase of the buffaloe. Their language is very guttural and difficult, and superstitious ceremonies and customs prevail amongst them which are similar to those observed by the Tartars. The Sioux, like the Tartars, sometimes offer water as a symbol of peace and safety to a stranger, or of pardon to an offender, which strongly corroborates the idea that they were originally from Asia. Some time ago I was informed by an officer, who had numbers of them under his influence in the American war, that a Sioux Indian was doomed to die for an offence which he had committed, and taking his station before the tribe, and drawing his blanket over his face, in expectation of the fatal shot, the Chief stepped forward and presented some water to him, as a token of pardon, when he was permitted again to join the party. They consider it also as a very bad omen in common with the Tartars, to cut a stick that has been burnt by fire, and with them they consign every thing to destruction, though it be their canoe, as polluted, if it be sprinkled with the water of animals. And it is a remarkable fact, that the laws of separation and uncleanness, being forty days for a male child and eighty for a female, observed by these Indians, exactly correspond with the Levitical law imposed upon the Jews in the birth of their children.

They are truly barbarous, like the Indians in general, towards their captive enemies. The following circumstance, as related to me by an Indian woman, whom I married to one of the principal settlers, and who was a near relation of one of the women who was tomahawked by a war party of Sioux Indians, some time ago, is calculated to fill the mind with horror. They fell upon four lodges belonging to the Saulteaux, who had encamped near *Fond du Lac*, Lake Superior, and which contained the wives and children of about twelve men, who were at that time absent a hunting; and immediately killed and scalped the whole party, except one woman and two or three of the children. With the most wanton and savage cruelty, they proceeded to put one of these little ones to death, by first turning him for a short time close before a fire, when they cut off one of his arms, and told him to run; and afterwards cruelly tortured him, with the other children, till he died.

It is almost incredible the torture to which they will sometimes put their prisoners; and the adult captives will endure it without a tear or a groan. In spite of all their sufferings, which the love of cruelty and revenge can invent and inflict upon them, they continue to chaunt their death song with a firm voice; considering that to die like a man, courting pain rather than flinching from it, is the noblest triumph of the warrior. In going to war, some time ago, a Sioux chief cut a piece of flesh from his thigh, and holding it up with a view to animate and encourage the party who were to accompany him to the ferocious conflict, told them to see how little he regarded pain, and that, despising torture and the scalping knife and tomahawk of their enemies, they should rush upon them, and pursue them till they were exterminated; and thereby console the spirits of the dead whom they had slain.

It does not appear that cannibalism is practised by any of the North American Indians; on the contrary, the eating of human flesh is held in great abhorrence by them: and when they are driven to eat it, through dire necessity, they are generally shunned by other Indians who know it, and who often take their lives secretly. It is not an uncommon practice, however, for them to cut flesh from their captives, and, when cooked to eat small bits of it, as well as to give some to their children, with a little of their blood, no doubt under the idea that it will give them courage, and a spirit of hatred and revenge against their enemies. What can calm these ferocious feelings, and curb this savage fury of the passions in the torturous destruction of defenceless women and sucking infants? what, but the introduction and influence of Christianity, the best civilizer of the wandering natives of these dreary wilds, and the most probable means of fixing them in the pursuit of agriculture, and of those social advantages and privileges to which they are at present strangers.

May 24.—By the arrival of the boats from Qu'appelle, I received another little Indian boy for admission into the school; and felt encouraged in the persuasion, that should we extend our travels among the Indians, and make known to them our simple object in visiting them as Missionaries, many probably among the different tribes who traded at the Company's Posts, would be gradually led to give up their children for education. I had now several under my care, who could converse pretty freely in English, and were beginning to read tolerably well, repeating the Lord's prayer correctly. The *primary* object in teaching them, was to give them a *religious* education; but the use of the bow was not to be forgotten, and they were hereafter to be engaged in hunting, as opportunities and circumstances might allow. As agriculture was an important branch in the system of instruction, I had given them some small portions of ground to cultivate; and I never saw European schoolboys more delighted than they were, in hoeing and planting their separate gardens. Nor were the parents of these boys insensible to the care and kindness that were shewn to them. I was told by one of the

Company's officers, that before he left Qu'appelle for the colony, he saw the father of the boy I had received from the Indian tents, after my visit to that quarter, and asked him to part with a fine horse that he was riding, which he refused to do, saying that he kept it for the ""Black Robe,"" a name by which they distinguished me from the Catholic priests, whom they call the ""Long Robe,"" for taking care of his boy. He repeated his application for the horse, with the tempting offer of some rum; but the Indian was firm in his intention of keeping it, as a present for kindness shewn to his child. This was gratitude; and I left directions, in my absence from the Settlement, that should he bring it down, he should be treated with all possible kindness; and amply repaid with blankets, or any useful European articles that he might want and which could be procured, in return for the gift of his horse.

It was now hinted to me, that the interest I was taking in the education of the native children, had already excited the fears of some of the chief factors and traders, as to the extent to which it might be carried. Though a few conversed liberally with me on the subject, there were others who were apprehensive that the extension of knowledge among the natives, and the locating them in agricultural pursuits, where practicable, would operate as an injury to the fur trade. My reply on the contrary was, that if Christian knowledge were gradually diffused among the natives throughout the vast territory of the Hudson's Bay Company, from the shores of the Atlantic to those of the North Pacific, it would best promote the honour and advantages of all parties concerned in the fur trade, and which I was persuaded was the general enlightened opinion of the Directors in London.

The 28th. The Settlers have been busily employed of late in getting in their seed corn, and much more has been sown than was expected a short time ago, from the prudent management of the grain, by the Chargè d'Affaires of the Colony, in the dearth of provisions; and from the supply which we have received from *Bas la Rivière*. The sturgeon season also has been very successful, which has in some measure brightened the countenances of a people, who have passed a long and severe winter, without ""*the sound of the mill stones, and the light of the candle*.""

CHAPTER IV.

ARRIVAL OF CANOE FROM MONTREAL. LIBERAL PROVISION FOR MISSIONARY ESTABLISHMENT. MANITOBAH LAKE. INDIAN GARDENS. MEET CAPTAIN FRANKLIN AND OFFICERS OF THE ARCTIC EXPEDITION, AT YORK FACTORY. FIRST ANNIVERSARY OF THE AUXILIARY BIBLE SOCIETY. HALF-CASTE CHILDREN. AURORA BOREALIS. CONVERSATION WITH PIGEWIS. GOOD HARVEST AT THE SETTLEMENT, AND ARRIVAL OF CATTLE FROM UNITED STATES MASSACRE OF HUNTERS. PRODUCE OF GRAIN AT THE COLONY.

On the 20th of June, the light canoe arrived from Montreal, which brought me letters from England; and no one ever received news from a far country, which gladdened the heart more than these letters did mine. My family were all well; and a liberal provision had been made, for a Missionary establishment at the Red River, for the maintenance and education of native Indian children, by the Church Missionary Society. In conveying this information to me, an active friend to the communication of Christianity to the Indians, observes, ""I hope a foundation is now laid to extend the blessings of Christianity, religion, morals, and education, wherever the representative of the Company may set his foot."" God grant that if may! and that the Light which first sprang up in Judea, may break forth upon every part of these vast territories, dissipate the present darkness of the natives, and lead them to the enjoyment of ""*the fulness of the blessings of the gospel of Christ*.""

All, all, is encouraging to proceed: yet I will not conceal my fears, that expectations may be raised too high, as to the progress that may be made in that vast field of labour which presents itself.—""There are a great many willows to cut down, and roots to remove,"" as an Indian chief said to me, when he welcomed me to the country, ""before the path will be clear to walk in."" The axe, however, is laid to the root of the tree, in the establishment of schools, as the means of instruction and of diffusing Christian knowledge in this moral wilderness; and we may anticipate the hope that numbers will arise to enjoy what they are capable of feeling, the endearments of social life, as well as of moral and religious education.

Soon after the express canoe arrived, a Director of the Hudson's Bay Company and an executor of the late Earl of Selkirk, came to the Settlement, via Montreal. I accompanied him to Pembina; and he acted upon the opinion, that the inhabitants of this distant and extreme point of the colony, who were principally hunters, were living too near the supposed line of demarcation, between the British territories and the United States; and that it would be far better for them to remove down to the Forks; where, if the industry of the colonists was more concentrated, it would tend more to their protection and prosperity. Many promised to comply with this suggestion. On our return, I took the opportunity of opening, with divine service, the building (though it was not finished) which was intended as a school-house, and a temporary place for divine worship; and, at the same time, baptized two of the boys who had been under my charge, one as James Hope, and the other as Henry Budd; they being able to read the New Testament, repeat the Church Catechism, and to understand the chief truths of the Christian Religion.

July 18.—We have the satisfaction of seeing the new sown grain promise well for a crop; and great hopes are entertained that it will this year escape the ravages of the locusts. Under this sanguine expectation, I left the colony, with the Director, on the 22d, on my annual visit to York Factory, taking the route of Manitobah Lake. As we passed this fine and extensive sheet of water, we saw occasionally some beautiful points, or bluffs of wood and the most striking and romantic scenery that can be presented to the eye. The waters abound with fish; and the alluvial soil of some parts, near the banks of the lake, promises every encouragement to the active industry of the agriculturist. A tribe of Indians, who traverse this part of the country, have gardens, in which they grow potatoes and pumpkins; and were encouragement given them, by the presence and superintendence of a Missionary, in the cultivation of the soil, and the assistance of a plough and seed corn, afforded them from the Colony, with the view to establish them in a village, there is little doubt, that they would gradually, or indeed soon, become so far civilized, as to promote the formation of a school among them for the education of their children. We proceeded on our way, through the Dauphin River, into Lake Winipeg, and arrived at Norway House, in about a week after we left the Settlement.

When within about fifty miles of York Fort, two Indians paddled their canoe to the side of the boat, and requested that I would take a little boy, who was with them, under my charge. This I consented to do, if they would bring him to me on my return to the Colony; and I threw him a blanket, as he was almost naked, and suffering apparently from cold. In landing at the Factory, I had the pleasure of meeting Captain Franklin, and the gentlemen of the Northern Land Expedition, recently returned from their arduous journey to the mouth of the Coppermine River, and waiting for the return of the Company's ship to England. An Esquimaux Indian, who accompanied the expedition as one of the guides, named Augustus, and who survived the supposed fate of his companion, Junius,[6] often came to my room, and interested me with his conversation in English, which was tolerably well understood by him, from the instructions he had received during his travels. He belongs to a tribe that annually visits Churchill Factory, from the northward; and often assures me, that ""Esquimaux want white man to come and teach them;"" and tells me, that they would ""make snow house, good, properly, for him in winter; and bring plenty of musk oxen and deer for him to eat."" Captain Franklin expressed much interest for this harmless race of Indians: and having spoken to the Governor of this northern district, I have resolved upon visiting Churchill, next July, in the hope of meeting the tribe on their visit to that Factory, and to obtain information, as to the practicability of sending a schoolmaster amongst them, or forming a school for the education of their children.

During my stay at the Factory, we held the first anniversary meeting of the Auxiliary Bible Society, and were warmly assisted by Captain Franklin and the gentlemen of the expedition. It appeared that the amount of donations and annual subscriptions for the past year, i.e. from Sept. 2nd, 1821, when the Society was first formed, to Sept. 2nd, 1822, was 200*l.* 0*s.* 6*d.* the whole of which sum was remitted to the parent institution in London; and the very encouraging sum of sixty pounds was subscribed at the meeting, towards the collection for the second year.

There were but few persons who came out by the ship for the Colony this year, as the succession of difficulties we had met with, had lessened the encouragement to emigrate to this quarter. Among those who came, however, was a young woman, as the intended wife of the schoolmaster, who was appointed by the Church Missionary Society, to assist in teaching at the Mission Establishment at Red River. I obtained a little boy and girl from an Indian tent at the Factory, to accompany her, in addition to those who were already there. The features of the boy bore a strong resemblance to those of the Esquimaux: but there was a shade of difference between the little girl, and Indians of entire blood, which was particularly seen in the colour of her hair. It was not of that jet black, which is common with the Indians in general, and which is the case with many of the children belonging to the tribes, or individual families who visit, or are much about the different Factories. I often met with half-caste children, whose parents had died or deserted them; who are growing up with numbers at the different posts in great depravity. Should their education be neglected, as it has hitherto been, and should they be led to ""*find their grounds,*"" with the Indians, it cannot be a matter of surprise, if at any time hereafter they should collectively or in parties, threaten the peace of the country, and the safety of the trading Posts.

Sept. 4.—The Indians who brought the boy in the canoe to the boat on my way to the Factory met me on my return, and he is taking his passage with the other two children to the Settlement. Though I have now made the voyage several times from York Fort to the Colony, I do not find that the labour and difficulty of the way are at all relieved. Some parts of the tracking ground might evidently be improved by cutting away the willows at the edges of the river; and the track over a few of the portages might also be made better; some of the large stones likewise might be removed when the water is low, which is expeditiously done by digging a large hole by the side and undermining them; when they are rolled over and buried. But to improve the passage materially, appears to me to be impracticable, from the shallowness of the water, and the rapidity of the current in many of the rivers. We saw that beautiful phenomenon called the '*Aurora Borealis,*' or the northern lights, on most clear evenings, consisting of long columns of clear white light, shooting across the heavens with a tremulous motion, and altering slowly to a variety of shapes. At times they were very brilliant, and appeared suddenly in different parts of the sky, where none had been seen before. It has been observed, that this phenomenon is not vivid in very high latitudes, and that its seat appears to be about the latitude of 60°#176;.

Many of the Indians have a pleasing and romantic idea of this meteor. They believe the northern lights to be the spirits of their departed friends dancing in the clouds, and when they are remarkably bright, at which time they vary most in form and situation, they say that their deceased friends are making merry.

The northern Indians call the Aurora Borealis ""Edthin, i.e. Deer, from having found that when a hairy deer-skin is briskly stroked with the hand in a dark night, it will emit many sparks of electrical fire as the back of a cat will.""

On the 5th of October we reached the encampment of Pigewis, the chief of the Red River Indians; and on pitching our tents for the night a little way farther up on the banks of the river, he came with his eldest son and another Indian and drank tea with me in the evening. It was the first time that I had met with him, since I received the encouraging information from the Church Missionary Society, relative to the Mission School at the Colony, and I was glad of the opportunity of assuring him, through the aid of an interpreter, who was of our party, ""that many, very many in my country wished the Indians to be taught white man's knowledge of the Great Spirit, and as a proof of their love to them, my countrymen had told me to provide for the clothing, maintenance, and education of many of their children; and had sent out the young person whom he then saw to teach the little girls who might be sent to the school for instruction."" Though not easily persuaded that you act from benevolent motives; he said *it was good!* and promised to tell all his tribe what I said about the children, and that I should have two of his boys to instruct in the Spring, but added, that 'the Indians like to have time to consider about these matters.' We smoked the calumet, and after pausing a short time, he shrewdly asked me what I would do with the children after they were taught what I wished them to know. I told him they might return to their parents if they wished it, but my hope was that they would see the advantage of making gardens, and cultivating the soil, so as not to be exposed to hunger and starvation, as the Indians generally were, who had to wander and hunt for their provisions. The little girls, I observed, would be taught to knit, and make articles of clothing to wear, like those which white people wore; and all would be led to read the Book that the Great Spirit had given to them, which the Indians had not yet known, and which would teach them how to live well and to die happy. I added, that it was the will of the Great Spirit, which he had declared in His Book, 'that a man should have but one wife, and a woman but one husband.' He smiled at this information, and said that 'he thought that there was no more harm in Indians having two wives than one of the settlers,' whom he named. I grieved for the depravity of Europeans as noticed by the heathen, and as raising a stumbling block in the way of their receiving instruction, and our conversation closed upon the subject by my observing, that 'there were some very bad white people, as there were some very bad Indians, but that the good book condemned the practice.'

We had an unusually fine passage from the Factory; and in our approach to Fort Douglas, we were cheered with the sight of several stacks of corn standing near to some of the settlers houses, and were informed, not only of a good harvest, but also of more than a hundred and fifty head of cattle having arrived at the colony, from the Illinois territory. These were encouraging circumstances, and I saw with peculiar pleasure, a stack of wheat near the Mission School, which had been raised, with nearly two hundred bushels of potatoes, from the ground that we had cultivated near it; and having purchased two cows for the establishment, our minds were relieved from anxiety as to provisions for the children during the winter, as well as from the quantity of grain that might be collected, till another harvest. Our fears were kept alive however, as to the safety of the Settlement, by being informed of another horrid massacre of four hunters, a woman, and a little girl, on the plains near Pembina, by the Sioux Indians. Their bodies were dreadfully mangled, and the death of the little girl was attended with atrocious barbarity. When the Indians first approached and made their attack on the party, she concealed herself under one of the carts; but hearing the screams of her friends as the savages were butchering them, she ran from the place of her concealment, and was shot through with an arrow as she was running to escape. The frequent massacre of the hunters by the Sioux Indians, and the constant alarm excited at the Settlement, by reports that they would come down with the savage intention of scalping us call for some military protection. A small party stationed at the Colony, would not only be the means of enforcing any civil process in the punishment of delinquents among the Colonists, but afford that security in their habitations, which would stimulate them to make improvements, and to a more active industry upon the soil, while it would have the best effect upon the minds of the Indians at large.

Nov. 4.—A party of hunters have just returned, bringing in some venison of the red deer, or stag, which is sometimes killed at the distance of about ten or twelve miles from the Colony. It is astonishing with what keenness of observation they pursue these animals: their eye is so very acute, that they will often discern a path, and trace the deer over the rocks and the withered leaves, which an European passes without noticing, or being at all aware, that any human being or game have directed their course before him. They distinguish the cardinal points by the terms, sun-rise, sun-set, cold country, and warm country; and reach any destined point over the most extensive plains with great accuracy, or travel through the thickest woods with certainty, when they have nothing to direct them but the moss that grows on the north side of the trunks of the trees, and their tops bending towards the rising sun.

The 18th. The attendance on divine worship is much improved on the Sabbath, from the accommodation the building affords, and I hope to complete it in the ensuing spring. We have a considerable number of half-caste children, and some adult Indian women, married to Europeans, who attend a Sunday-school, for gratuitous instruction; and I have no doubt that their numbers will increase considerably in the spring. These children have capacity, and would rival Europeans, with the like instruction, in the developement of their mental faculties. Extensive plans might be devised, and carried into effect, if patronized by an active co-operation, which would ultimately result in producing great benefits to the half-caste population, and the Indians in general. There is an opening for schools on the banks of the Saskashawan, where the soil is good for cultivation, as well as on the banks of the Athabasca river; and frequent applications reached me to forward their establishment in those quarters, under the prospect of their being supported through the produce that might be raised from the soil, and the supplies to be obtained from the waters and the chase.

The winter has again set in, and many of the settlers are threshing out their crops; and from the best information I can obtain, the return of wheat has been from twenty to twenty-five bushels per acre. Barley, may be stated at the same produce: but where sown in small quantities, and under particular cultivation, I have heard of thirty, forty, and fifty fold being reaped. Taking the average of the general crop, however, I think it may be fairly stated at the above increase, without the trouble of manuring. That useful article of food, the potatoe thrives well, and returns upon an average thirty bushels for one. Indian corn is grown; and every kind of garden vegetable, with water melons, and pumpkins, comes to great perfection, when spared by the locusts. Some have raised the tobacco plant, but it has not yet met with a fair trial, any more than the sowing of hemp and flax. I failed in the experiment of sowing some winter wheat, which I brought with me from England; but I attribute this failure, to its being sown in an exposed situation, and too early in the autumn, the plant having been of too luxuriant a growth, before the severe frosts came on.—If sown in sheltered spots, and later in the season, there is every probability of its surviving the winter, which would be of great advantage in agriculture, from the short period we have for preparing the land and sowing it in spring. We have no fruit trees, but if introduced, they would no doubt thrive at the Colony. We get a few raspberries in the woods, and strawberries from the plains in summer; and on the route to York Factory, we meet with black and red currants, gooseberries, and cranberries. There is a root which is found in large quantities, and generally called by the settlers, the Indian potatoe. It strongly resembles the Jerusalem artichoke, and is eaten by the natives in a raw state; but when boiled it is not badly flavoured. The characteristic improvidence of the Indians, and their precarious means of subsistence, will often reduce them to extreme want, and I have seen them collecting small roots in the swamps, and eating the inner rind of the poplar tree, and having recourse to a variety of berries, which are found in abundance in many parts of the country.

CHAPTER V.

CLIMATE OF RED RIVER. THERMOMETER. PIGEWIS'S NEPHEW. WOLVES. REMARKS OF GENERAL WASHINGTON. INDIAN WOMAN SHOT BY HER SON. SUFFERINGS OF INDIANS. THEIR NOTIONS OF THE DELUGE. NO VISIBLE OBJECT OF ADORATION. ACKNOWLEDGE A FUTURE LIFE. LEFT THE COLONY FOR BAS LA RIVIÈRE;. LOST ON WINIPEG LAKE. RECOVER THE TRACK, AND MEET AN INTOXICATED INDIAN. APPARENT FACILITIES FOR ESTABLISHING SCHOOLS WEST OF ROCKY MOUNTAINS. RUSSIANS AFFORDING RELIGIOUS INSTRUCTION ON THE NORTH WEST COAST OF NORTH AMERICA. RUMOURS OF WAR AMONG THE SURROUNDING TRIBES WITH THE SIOUX INDIANS.

January 1, 1823.—Once more I have to record the goodness of God in preserving my life, and granting me the invaluable blessing of health throughout the past year.

> ""God of my life! to thee belong
>
> The thankful heart, the grateful song.""

May my days be spent with renewed ardour and watchfulness in my Christian profession; never yielding to supineness and discouragements in my Ministerial labours, and toils in the wilderness. Of all men, the Missionary most needs strong faith, with a simple reliance upon the providence and promises of God in the trials that await him. His path is indeed an arduous one. Many unexpected circumstances will oppose his conscientious endeavours to fulfil his calling; and difficulties will surround him in every shape, so as to put his patience, his hopes of usefulness and steady perseverance severely to the test. He will often exclaim in the deep conviction of his mind, who is sufficient for the great undertaking?—Experience in the Missionary field has convinced me, that there are indeed but *few among a thousand* qualified for the difficult and exalted work. If that eminent Missionary, St. Paul, abounding in zeal, and in all the graces of the Spirit, thought it needful to solicit the prayers of the Churches that ""the word of the Lord might run, and have free course,"" how earnest ought our entreaties to be of all friends of missions to ""pray for us,"" who, *if we feel aright*, must feel our own insignificance, in our labours among the heathen, and in our services to the Christian church, when compared with the labours of the Apostles, or with those of a Swartz, a Brainerd, or a Martyn.

The climate of Red River is found to be remarkably healthy, and the state of the weather may be pretty accurately ascertained from the following table for the last two years. We know of no epidemic, nor is a cough scarcely ever heard amongst us. The only cry of affliction, in breathing a sharp pure air, that creates a keen appetite, has been, '*Je n'ai rien pour manger*,' and death has rarely taken place amongst the inhabitants, except by accident and extreme old age. It is far otherwise, however with the natives of the country, who from the hardships and incessant toil they undergo in seeking provisions, look old at forty, and the women at a much earlier age: while numbers die, at an early stage of their suffering existence, of pulmonary consumptions. These are so common, that they may be considered as the unavoidable consequence of privations and immoderate fatigue, which they endure in hunting and in war; and of being continually exposed to the inclemency of the seasons.

CLIMATE OF RED RIVER

THERMOMETER.

Month and Year	Date	A.M. Below °	A.M. Above °	M. Below °	M. Above °	A.M. Below °	P.M. Above °	Average Below °	Average Above °
1821.									
January	23	24	..	16	..	26	..	22	..
February	2	30	..	25	..	28	..	28	..
March	17	5	..	..	13	5	..	..	1
April	9	..	10	..	18	..	17	..	15
May	8	..	50	..	77	..	77	..	68
June	3	..	72	..	84	..	88	..	81
July	28	..	76	..	91	..	90	..	85
August	3	..	70	..	84	..	88	..	84

September	4	..	58	..	68	..	70	..	65
October	25	..	45	..	62	..	65	..	27
November	26	5	..	16	..	16	..	12	..
December	17	38	..	15	..	16	..	23	..
1822.									
January	28	34	..	25	..	25	..	28	..
February	3	32	..	19	..	23	..	25	..
March	13	..	7	..	25	..	10	..	14
April	8	..	5	..	18	..	21	..	15
May	28	..	65	..	77	..	78	..	73
June	9	..	68	..	76	..	76	..	73
July	21	..	75	..	87	..	81	..	81
August	8	..	74	..	83	..	84	..	80
September	13	..	59	..	79	..	78	..	72
October	4	..	54	..	72	..	71	..	66
November	29	24	..	2	..	15	..	14	..
December	14	49	..	25	..	28	..	34	..

I have selected the day in each month of the year, when the thermometer was at the lowest and highest degree of Zero; which will give a general idea of the change of the state of the air. Though I have been informed of the thermometer having been several degrees higher and lower at the Colony, than here stated, the winter is nearly the same, as to the time it sets in and breaks up, as that of Montreal; but the frost is rather more intense, with less snow, and a clearer air. During the winter months, a north-westerly wind, which is synonymous in this quarter of the globe, with excessive cold, generally prevails; and even in sultry weather, the moment that the wind veers from the south to that quarter, its chilling influence is immediately felt in the sudden transition from heat to cold. In summer, a southerly wind blows commonly with considerable heat, and often in heavy gales, is accompanied with violent torrents of rain, and much thunder.

The 4th.—The Indians around us generally divide into small parties for the better support of their families during the winter months; and in their rambling existence in search of animals for provisions. Pigewis and a few others, occupying two lodges, called on me to-day, saying that they were starving. The woods which they generally hunted were burnt to a great extent during the last autumn, and they had only killed a bear, and a few martins, with occasionally a rabbit, as a subsistence for the last two months. This was their report, though they often deceive in their lounging habits of begging at your residence. I assisted them with a little Indian rice and some potatoes, on their promise to strike their tents, and proceed to some other hunting grounds on the following day. When they visit under these destitute circumstances, they are often exceedingly troublesome, acknowledging no right of restraint in being shut out from your presence; they enter your dwelling without ceremony, and covet almost every thing that they see. With a view, therefore, to keep them from my room in the evening, I sent some tea and sugar with a little flour, for the purpose of taking my tea with them in one of their tents. I was accompanied by one of the Indian boys from the school as an interpreter, who now acted well in that capacity, from the great progress he had made in speaking English, and found them all encircling a small fire, by the side of which they had placed a buffaloe robe for me to sit down upon. The pipe was immediately lighted by an Indian whom we generally call 'Pigewis's Aid-de-Camp;' and having pointed the stem to the heavens and then to the earth, he gave the first whiff to the Master of Life, and afterwards handed it to me. Pigewis then delivered what I understood to be an address to the Great Spirit, and the party seated around him used an expression, apparently of assent, in the middle and conclusion of his speech. Though addressing an unknown God, what a reflection does his conduct, in returning thanks for his short and precarious supplies, to the Master of Life, cast upon multitudes who profess Christianity and the knowledge of the true God, and yet daily partake of the bounties of his providence, without any expression of gratitude, or whose only return, is to live in the known violation of his laws, and to blaspheme his holy name, in the midst of his goodness towards them!

Pigewis breakfasted with me on the following morning; and his general remarks in conversation gave me, as they had done before, a favourable opinion of his penetration and mental ability. The active efforts of his mind, however, are confined principally to those objects which immediately affect his present wants or enjoyments. Savages talk of the animals that they have killed, and boast of the scalps that they have taken in their war excursions; but they form no arrangement, nor enter into calculation for futurity. They have no settled place of abode, or property, or acquired wants and appetites, like those which rouse men to activity in civilized life, and stimulate them to persevering industry, while they keep the mind in perpetual exercise and ingenious invention. Their simple wants are few, and when satisfied they waste their time in listless indolence; and are often seen lying on the ground for whole days together, without raising their heads from under the blanket, or uttering a single word. The cravings of hunger rouse them; and the scarcity of animals that now prevails in many parts of the country, is a favourable circumstance towards leading them to the cultivation of the soil; which would expand their minds, and prove of vast advantage, among other means, in aiding their comprehension of Christianity. It must, not be expected, however, that the Indians will easily forsake a mode of life that is so congenial to man, in his natural love of ease and indolence and licentious freedom. Necessity, in a measure, must compel them to do this; *but the children may be educated, and trained to industry upon the soil*, in the hope that they may be recovered from their savage habits and customs, to see and enjoy the blessings of civilization and Christianity. This object is highly important, and no means should be spared in attempting its accomplishment, where practicable. Where is our humanity and Christian sympathy, and how do we fulfil the obligations which Christianity has enforced, if we do not seek to raise these wandering heathen, who, with us, are immortal in their destiny, from a mere animal existence to the partaking of the privileges and hopes of the Christian religion?

Before Pigewis left me, his sister arrived, who was then living with a very lazy bad Indian, and asked me to take her eldest boy, whose father was dead, into the school. Though much above the usual age of admission upon the establishment, I consented to receive him; and they both took an affectionate leave of him, remarking that they were sure I should keep him well. The whole party then set off towards some fresh hunting grounds, and it was my hope and expectation that I should see nothing more of them till the spring. The boy was comfortably clothed, and he appeared to be well satisfied with the rest at the school, and had begun to learn the English alphabet, when, to my surprise, I found the mother, with the Indian, in my room, in about a week after they had left the Settlement with Pigewis, saying that they had parted from him in consequence of their not being able to obtain any provision; and that ""they thought it long"" since they had seen the boy. He was permitted to go from the school-house to their tent, which they had pitched near me in the woods, almost daily without restraint, till at length he refused to return. I repeated my request for him without effect; and having my suspicion excited, that they would take him away for the sake of the clothing and blankets which I had given him, I determined upon having them again, as an example to deter others from practising the like imposition. The parties were angry at my determination, and looking upon the medicine bag that was suspended on the willows near the tent, and which is carried by most of the Indians, as a sacred depository for a few pounded roots, some choice bits of earth, or a variety of articles which they only know how to appreciate with superstitious regard, they told me that ""they had bad medicine for those who displeased them."" I insisted, however, on the return of the articles I had given to the boy, and obtained them; at the same time promising that if he would go back to the school-house, he should have his clothes again; but added, that ""it would never be allowed for Indians to bring their children to the school, which was established to teach them what was for their happiness, merely for the purpose of getting them clothed and provided with blankets, and then to entice them to leave it.""

Jan. 20.—The severity of the winter has driven a number of wolves to hover about the Settlement in search of provisions; they are perfectly harmless however, as they are met singly, and skulk away like a dog conscious of having committed a theft. But in packs, they kill the horses, and are formidable to encounter. In the pursuit of buffaloes and the deer on the plains, they are known to form a crescent, and to hurry their prey over precipices, or upon the steep muddy banks of a river, where they devour them. No instance has occurred of their having seized any of the children of the settlers, though they sometimes kill and eat the carcases of the dogs close to their houses.

February 3.—It appears that I have given great offence to one of the remaining Swiss emigrants, for refusing to baptize, at his immediate request, the child of his daughter, born of fornication, and cast away by her, as living in adultery. I deeply lamented the circumstance, but felt the obligation to defer the administration of the sacrament, from the conviction that the profligacy of the case called for an example which might deter others among the Swiss from acting in the like manner; and at the same time be a public expression of disapprobation, on my part, of such unblushing depravity, in the eyes of a numerous young people growing up at the Colony. Unless chastity be considered as a virtue, what hope can be entertained of forming any organized society? and if the Colonists fearlessly commit crimes, because they have stepped over a certain line of latitude; and live in a wild profligacy, without the curb of civil restraint, the Settlement can hold out but faint hopes of answering in any way the expectations of its patrons. Till morality and religion form its basis, disappointment must follow. Nor can I imagine that the system taught by the Canadian Catholic priests will avail any thing materially in benefitting the morals of the people; they are bigotted to opinions which are calculated to fetter the human mind, to cramp human exertion, and to keep their dependants in perpetual leading-strings. Their doctrine is—

""Extra Ecclesiam Romanam, salus non esse potest.""[7]

They appear to me to teach Christianity only as a dry system of ecclesiastical statutes, without a shadow of spirituality. While they multiply holidays, to the interruption of human industry, as generally complained of by those who employ Canadians, they lightly regard the Sabbath; and sanction the practice of spending the evenings of this sacred day at cards, or in the dance. In their tinkling service of worshipping the elevated host as the very God himself, they fall down also in adoration to the Virgin Mary, addressing her, as—

> ""Reine des Cieux!
>
> Intercedez pour nous,
>
> Mère de Dieu!""

and proudly arrogate to the Church of Rome, the absolute interpretation of Scripture; forbidding the people to examine whether she does it rightly or not. I thank God that I am a Protestant against such idolatry and ecclesiastical tyranny!

The able and enlightened remarks of that renowned general and eminent statesman, Washington, in his farewell address to the people of the United States, relative to the well-being of a nation, are equally applicable to the existence and prosperity of a Colony: ""Of all the dispositions and habits which lead to political prosperity (he observed), religion and morality are indispensable supports. In vain would that man claim the tribute of patriotism, who should labour to subvert these great pillars of human happiness, these firmest props of men and citizens. The mere politician, equally with the pious man, ought to respect and cherish them. A volume would not trace all their connexions with private and public felicity. Let it be simply asked, Where is the security for property, for reputation, for life, if the sense of religious obligation desert the oaths which are the instruments of investigation in the courts of justice? And let us with caution indulge the supposition, that morality can be maintained without religion. Whatever be conceded to the influence of refined education, or minds of a peculiar structure; reason and experience forbid us to expect that national morality can prevail in exclusion of religious principle.""

A daughter has driven her aged Indian father, lashed, in his buffaloe robe, on a sledge, to the Colony. He appeared to be in a very weak and dying state, and has suffered much from the want of provisions. I was much pleased with this instance of filial affection and care. Sometimes the aged and infirm are abandoned or destroyed; and however shocking it may be to those sentiments of tenderness and affection, which in civilized life we regard as inherent in our common nature, it is practised by savages in their hardships and extreme difficulty of procuring subsistence for the parties who suffer, without being considered as an act of cruelty, but as a deed of mercy. This shocking custom, however, is seldom heard of among the Indians of this neighbourhood; but is said to prevail with the Chipewyan or Northern Indians, who are no sooner burdened with their relations, broken with years and infirmities, and incapable of following the camp, than they leave them to their fate. Instead of repining they are reconciled to this dreadful termination of their existence, from the known custom of their nation, and being conscious that they can no longer endure the various distresses and fatigue of savage life, or assist in hunting for provisions. A little meat, with an axe, and a small portion of tobacco, are generally left with them by their *nearest relations*, who in taking leave of them, say, that it is time for them to go into the other world, which they suppose lies just beyond the spot where the sun goes down, where they will be better taken care of than with them, and then they walk away weeping. On the banks of the Saskashawan, an aged woman prevailed on her son to shoot her through the head, instead of adopting this sad extremity. She addressed him in a most pathetic manner, reminding him of the care and toil with which she bore him on her back from camp to camp in his infancy; with what incessant labour she brought him up till he could use the bow and the gun; and having seen him a great warrior, she requested that he would shew her kindness, and give a proof of his courage, in shooting her, that she might go home to her relations. ""I have seen many winters, she added, and am now become a burden, in not being able to assist in getting provisions; and dragging me through the country, as I am unable to walk, is a toil, and brings much distress: — take your gun."" She then drew her blanket over her head, and her son immediately deprived her of life: in the apparent consciousness of having done an act of filial duty and of mercy.

The old man who was brought to the Settlement, by his daughter for relief soon recovered, so as to become exceedingly troublesome by coming almost daily to my room. I succeeded at length in starting them for some hunters' tents on the plains, where they expressed a wish to go, if supplied with provisions to carry them there, by killing a small dog, and giving it to them for food. An ox would not have been more acceptable to a distressed European family than this animal was to these Indians. But on leaving me two more families came to my residence in a state of starvation. Necessity had compelled them to eat their dogs, and they themselves were harnessed to their sledges, dragging them in a most wretched and emaciated condition. One of the men appeared to be reduced to the last stage of existence, and upon giving him a fish and a few cooked potatoes, such was his natural affection for his children, that, instead of voraciously devouring the small portion of food, he divided it into morsels, and gave it to them in the most affectionate manner. His children from their appearance had partaken of by far the largest share of that scanty supply which he had lately been able to obtain in hunting. They pitched their tents at a short distance below in the woods, and the poor man came to me next morning with the request that I would bleed him for a violent pain which he complained of in his side. This I refused to do, and gave him a note to the medical gentleman of the Colony, promising to call on him the next day. When I saw him I found that he had not delivered the note, but had bled himself in the foot with the flint from his gun, and spoke of having experienced considerable relief. The party were dreadfully distressed for provisions, and had actually collected at their tents the remains of a dog which had died, with part of the head of a horse, that had been starved to death in the severity of the winter, and which was the only part of the animal that was left by the wolves. The head of the dog was boiling in the kettle, and that of the horse was suspended over it, to receive the smoke of the fire in the preparation for cooking; while the children were busily employed in breaking some bones which they had picked up, with an axe, and which they were sucking in their raw state for their moisture. This was the suffering extremity not of lazy bad Indians, but of those who bore the character of good hunters, and were particularly careful of their families; and I fear it is the case of many more from the exhausted state of animals in the neighbourhood of Red River: and from the frequent fires that occur in the plains, which extend also to the destruction of the woods.

Towards the conclusion of the month we had another melancholy proof of the Indians suffering extreme want from the few animals that were to be met with during the winter. An Indian with his wife on their arrival gave me to understand that they had been without food for twenty days, and had lost their three children by starvation. Their appearance was that of a melancholy dejection, and I had my suspicions excited at the time that they had eaten them. This was confirmed afterwards by the bones and hands of one of the children being found near some ashes at a place where they said they had encamped, and suffered their misery. It appears that two of their children died from want, whom they cooked and eat, and that they afterwards killed the other for a subsistence in their dire necessity. I asked this Indian, as I did the other, whether from having suffered so much, it was not far better to do as the white people did and cultivate the ground; he said, ""Yes;"" and expressed a desire to do so if he could obtain tools, seed wheat and potatoes to plant. Though it is the character of the savage to tell you what he will do in future at your suggestion, to prevent the calamity which he may be suffering from want of food or the inclemency of the weather, and as soon as the season becomes mild, and the rivers yield him fish, or the woods and plains provisions, to forget all his sufferings, and to be as thoughtless and improvident as ever as to futurity; yet, I think that a successful attempt might be made by a proper superintendance, and a due encouragement to induce some of the Indians of this quarter to settle in villages, and to cultivate the soil. The voice of humanity claims this attention to them, under their almost incredible privations at times: but prejudices may exist in the country which prevent this desirable object being carried into effect. There was a time when the Indians themselves had begun to collect into a kind of village towards the mouth of the Red River, had cultivated spots of ground, and had even erected something of a lodge for the purpose of performing some of their unmeaning ceremonies of ignorance and heathenism, and to which the Indians of all the surrounding country were accustomed at certain seasons to repair; but fears were entertained that the natives would be diverted from hunting furs to idle ceremonies, and an effectual stop was put to all further improvement, by the spirit of opposition that then existed in the country between the two rival Fur Companies.

March 10.—The ringing of the Sabbath bell now collects an encouraging congregation; and some of us, I trust, could experimentally adopt the language of the Psalmist, in saying, ""I was glad when they said unto us, let us go into the house of the Lord."" — My earnest prayer to God is, that I may exercise a *spiritual* ministry; and faithfully preach those truths which give no hope to fallen man, but that which is founded on God's mercy in Christ. I often felt rejoiced in spirit in the prospect of doing good amidst the wild profligacy of manners that surrounded me, and of making known the doctrines and precepts of Christianity, where Christ had never before been named. Several adult married Indian women attended the Sunday School, with many half-caste children to be taught to read, and to receive religious instruction, which gave me an opportunity of ascertaining what the notions of the Indians were concerning the flood and the creation of the world. They appeared either to be ignorant, or unwilling to relate any traditionary stories that they might have as to the original formation of the world, but spoke of an universal deluge, which they said was commonly believed by all Indians. When the flood came and destroyed the world, they say that a very great man, called Wæsackoochack, made a large raft, and embarked with otters, beavers, deer, and other kinds of animals. After it had floated upon the waters for some time, he put out an otter, with a long piece of shagganappy or leathern cord tied to its leg, and it dived very deep without finding any bottom, and was drowned. He then put out a beaver, which was equally unsuccessful, and shared the same fate. At length he threw out a musk-rat, that dived and brought up a little mud in its mouth, which Wæsackoochack took, and placing in the palm of his hand, he blew upon it, till it greatly enlarged itself, and formed a good piece of the earth. He then turned out a deer that soon returned, which led him to suppose that the earth was not large enough, and blowing upon it again its size was greatly increased, so that a loom which he then sent out never returned. The new earth being now of a sufficient size, he turned adrift all the animals that he had preserved. He is supposed still to have some intercourse with and power over them as well as over the Indians, who pray to him to protect them and keep them alive. Sir Alexander Mackenzie, in speaking of the Chipewyan or Northern Indians, who traverse an immense track of country, to the north of the Athabasca lake, says, ""that the notions which these people entertain of the creation are of a singular nature. They believe that the globe was at first one vast and entire ocean, inhabited by no living creature except a mighty bird, whose eyes were fire, whose glances were lightning, and the clapping of whose wings was thunder. On his descending to the ocean, and touching it, the earth instantly arose, and remained on the surface of the waters. They have also a tradition amongst them, that they originally came from another country, inhabited by very wicked people, and had traversed a great lake, where they suffered much misery, it being always winter, with ice and deep snow. At the Copper-Mine River, where they made the first land, the ground was covered with copper. They believe also that in ancient times their ancestors lived till their feet were worn out with walking, and their throats with eating. They describe a deluge, when the waters spread over the whole earth, except the highest mountains, on the tops of which they preserved themselves."" There appears to be a general belief of a flood among all the tribes of this vast continent; and the Bible shews me from whence spring all those fables, and wild notions which they entertain; and which prevail in other parts of the heathen world upon these subjects. They are founded upon those events which the sacred scriptures record, and which have been corrupted by different nations, scattered and wandering through the globe as the descendants of Noah, without a written language. The Hindoo therefore in his belief that the earth was actually drawn up at the flood, by the tusks of a boar, and that it rests at this hour on the back of a tortoise: and the North American Indian in his wild supposition that Wæsackoochack, whose reputed father was a snake, formed the present beautiful order of creation after the deluge, by the help of a musk-rat, afford no inconsiderable proof that the Bible is of far greater antiquity than any other record extant in the world, and that it is indeed of divine origin. While its sacred page therefore informs and decides my judgment by the earliest historic information, may its principles influence my life in all Christian practice, and joyful expectation of the world to come, through faith in Him, whom it records as the Redeemer of mankind; and in whom believing ""there is neither barbarian, Scythian, bond, nor free.""

'One song employs all nations, and all sing,

Worthy the Lamb! for he was slain for us.

The dwellers in the vales and on the rocks

Shout to each other; and the mountain-tops,
From distant mountains catch the flying joy;
Till, nation after nation taught the strain,
Earth rolls the rapturous hosannah round.'

I could never discover that the Indians among whom I travelled had any thing like a visible object of adoration. Neither sun, moon, nor stars, appear to catch their attention as objects of worship. There is an impression upon their minds, of a Divine Being, whom they call the *Great Spirit*, whom they ignorantly address, and suppose to be too good even to punish them. Their general idea is, that they are more immediately under the influence of a powerful *Evil Spirit*. Experience has taught them this melancholy fact, in the trials, sufferings, afflictions, and multiform death which they undergo; and therefore their prayers are directed to him, when any severe calamity befalls them. To avert his displeasure, they often have recourse to superstitious practices, with the most childish credulity; and will drum and dance throughout a whole night, in the hope of bringing relief to the sick and dying. They know not that the great enemy of man's happiness and salvation, is a chained enemy, and a captive to Him who triumphed in his resurrection and ascension to glory, and under the control and permissive will of Him, whom they denominate Keetchee Manitou, or Great Spirit; and, consequently they are enslaved to all that is pitiable in ignorance and superstition. Acknowledging the being of a God, the uncultivated minds of these savages have led them to shrink from the thoughts of annihilation, and to look forward with hope to a future life. They have no idea however of intellectual enjoyments; but a notion prevails among them, that at death they arrive at a large river, on which they embark in a stone canoe; and that a gentle current bears them on to an extensive lake, in the centre of which is a most beautiful island, in the sight of which they receive their judgment. If they have died courageously in war, they are particularly welcomed in landing upon the island, where they, with skilful hunters, enjoy perpetual spring and plenty, and live with all the good in an eternal enjoyment of sensual pleasures. If they die with their hands imbrued with the blood of their countrymen, and are lazy bad characters, the stone canoe sinks with them, leaving them up to their chins in water, that they may for ever behold the happiness of the good, and struggle in vain to reach the island of bliss.

The 17th. I left the Colony in a cariole, to visit the Company's Post at Bas la Rivière; we stopped the night, near the mouth of the Red River, and crossed the point of Lake Winipeg, on the ice, the following day, in time to reach the Fort the same evening. It is pleasantly situated by a fine sheet of water; and is the way the canoes take their route to Fort William, Lake Superior, and Montreal. During my stay, the officer of the Post gave me the much admired fish of the country, called by the Indians, *tittameg*, and by the Americans, *white-fish*. Its usual weight is about three or four pounds; but it is caught in some of the lakes of a much larger size; and, with the sturgeon, is a principal article of food, and almost the only support of some of the establishments. Before I left, the officer was married to one of the best informed and most improved half-caste women I had seen. She was the daughter of one of the chief factors, who was particularly fond of his family; and afforded an instance of superiority of character among this class of people, from the care and instruction which she had received. The Mètifs, or, as they are sometimes called, Bois brulés, have displayed the most striking ability as steersmen of boats, through the most difficult rapids, and in the navigation of the rivers; and if advantages were given them in education, they have capacities of usefulness which might adorn the highest stations of civilized life. Of the moral degradation, however, of these people, in common with that of the Canadian voyageurs, it is difficult to exhibit an accurate picture. Suffice it to say, that it is a degradation which, in some respects, exceeds even that of the native Indian himself.

In starting from the Company's Post, on my return to the Colony, it was my hope that we should cross the point of Winipeg Lake to the mouth of the Red River, in one day, as we had done in our way thither; but about two o'clock in the afternoon, I perceived, as I was in the cariole, that the driver had mistaken his way. I told him of his error, but he persisted in the opinion that he was right, and drove on till the evening closed upon us, without his finding the entrance to the Red River. Night came on, and the dogs were exhausted with fatigue, which obliged us to stop, though not before one of them contrived to slip his head out of the collar. It happened that we were near some wood on the edge of the lake, but in reaching it we sank in soft drift snow up to the middle; and it was a considerable time before we could make our preparations for the night, under the spreading branches of a pine tree. We got but little rest from the small fire that we were able to make, and from our bad encampment. The next morning, I found that the driver was greatly embarrassed in his idea of our exact situation, and he led me throughout the day from one point of wood to another, over the ice, on the borders of the lake, in a directly contrary way to that in which we ought to have gone. We had no food for our dogs, and on coming to our encampment for the night, the animals were completely worn out with fatigue; and what added to our trials, was the loss of the flint, which the man dropped in the snow, the first time he attempted to strike the steel to kindle a fire. After some difficulty we succeeded, with a small gun-flint, which I found in my pocket, and we bivouacked upon the snow, before an insufficient fire, from the scanty wood we were able to collect. It was my wish to have divided the little provision that remained with the dogs, as they had eaten nothing for two days, and I considered them scarcely able to move with the cariole the next morning, at the same time intending to kill one of them the following evening, to meet our wants, should we not succeed in recovering our track. The driver assured me, however, that they would go another day without giving up. From the conversation I had with him, before we started on the following morning, I found that he had no knowledge of our situation on the extensive lake before us, and supposed that the Red River lay to the north, while I thought, from the course of the sun, that it was to the south, and insisted upon his taking that direction, which we did accordingly; and after a laborious and rather anxious day's toil, we saw some points of small and scattered willow bushes, like those which I knew to be near the entrance of the river. This providentially proved to be the case, otherwise our trials must have been great; the driver having become nearly snow-blind, and incapable of driving the dogs, and the weather becoming more intensely cold and stormy. It may easily be conceived what our feelings were, in recovering a right track, after wandering for several days upon an icy lake, among the intricate and similar appearances of numerous and small islands of pine. They were those, I trust, of sincere gratitude to God; and I often thought what a wretched wanderer was man in a guilty world, without the light of Christianity to guide, and its principle to direct his steps. Infidelity draws a veil around him, and shrouds all in darkness as to a future life. All, all is uncertainty before him, as the tempest-tossed mariner without a compass, and the wearied wandering traveller without a chart or guide. Let me then prize the scriptures more, which have ""God for their author, truth unmingled with error for their subject, and salvation for their end."" They are the fountains of interminable happiness, where he who hungers and thirsts after righteousness, may be satisfied; and when received in principle and in love, are a sure and unerring guide, through a wilderness of toil and suffering, to the habitations of the blessed, ""not made with hands, eternal in the heavens.""

As we passed along the river towards the Settlement, we met an intoxicated Indian, who had been drinking at the grave of his child, whom he had buried in the fall of the year. In going to the spot, I found that all the snow and the grass had been removed, and that a number of Indians, with Pigewis, had encircled the place where the body had been deposited; and, as is their custom, they smoked the calumet, wept, and sacrificed a little of what they possessed to the departed spirit of the child. They do this, under the idea that the deceased may want these articles in the world whither they are gone; and it is very affecting occasionally to hear the plaintive and mournful lamentations of the mother at the grave of her child, uttering in pitiful accents, ""Ah! my child, why did you leave me! Why go out of my sight so early! Who will nurse you and feed you in the long journey you have undertaken!"" The strength of natural affection will sometimes lead them to commit suicide, under the idea that they shall accompany the spirit, and nurse their departed child in the other world. This persuasion, that the spirits of the deceased want the same attendance in their new station as in the present life, is so deeply rooted in the minds of the Indians, that the *Carriers*, west of the Rocky Mountains, sometimes burn the widow; and a chief, on the North-West coast of America, sacrificed a human victim, who was a slave, on the death of his son. In some provinces of America, historians have mentioned that, upon the death of a Chief, a certain number of his wives, and of his slaves who had been taken in war, were put to death, and interred together with him, that he might appear with the same dignity in the world of spirits, and be waited upon by the same attendants. Some have solicited the honour to die, while others have fled, as marked for victims, under this cruel and superstitious practice.

April 4.—On my arrival at the Church Mission House for divine worship, a poor Indian widow with five children, asked me to admit two of the boys into the schools, which I immediately did, and particularly wished her to leave the two girls also, one about six, and the other eight years of age; but she would not comply with my request. The boys were very wild and troublesome, and often ran away from the school to their mother, who was generally living about the Settlement. They were getting at length however better reconciled, and had begun to be attached to the schoolmaster, when I was informed the Catholics were prejudicing her mind against the school; and that some of the women of that persuasion had told her, that I was collecting children from the Indians with the intention of taking them away to my country. This idea was spread amongst them, and an Indian calling at my residence told me that he would give his boy to the school, if I would not leave them, as he understood I intended to do. In vain did I tell him, that in going home to see my wife and children I should be glad to return and bring them with me, to assist me in teaching those of his country; and that on my going away, my brother Minister would come, and love, and take care of the Indian children as I did. He was not satisfied, and took his boy away with him, saying he must wait, and see what was to be done. The Saulteaux woman took her two boys away clandestinely, saying, as I was afterwards informed, that ""they would be all the same as dead to her, if what she had heard was true,"" and though I had not an opportunity of seeing her afterwards, she had the honesty to return the children's clothes which I had given to them. These circumstances with others that had occurred, convinced me that it would be far better to obtain children for the school, from a distance than from the Indians in the immediate neighbourhood of the Colony, as all those children who were under our charge, and whose parents were more remote, soon became reconciled to restraint, and were happy on the establishment. This desirable object might soon be obtained by visiting the different tribes of Indians, more especially were there a powerful interest excited in favour of the Native School Establishment at Red River, by the officers at the different Trading Posts.

In the attempt however to spread the knowledge of Christianity among the natives, it appears that the least expensive mode of proceeding and of ensuring the most extensive success for the Missionary is, to visit those parts of the country where they are stationary, and live in villages during the greater part of the year. He should direct his way and persevering attention towards the rocky mountains, and the Columbia. He may meet with difficulties and obstacles such as have tried the faith and patience of Missionaries in other parts of the heathen world, but let him persevere through the aid of the Company's officers, who may introduce him to the Indians trading at their respective Posts. Near to the foot of the rocky mountains the Indians are known to dwell in their villages nearly nine months of the year. During these months they live on salmon, either dried or taken fresh from the rivers. They are not ferocious, but very indolent, and where this is the case, are generally very licentious; but as they are stationary for so long a period, an attempt might be made through the co-operation of the Company's Officer, to lead them to cultivate the soil, which at certain points will grow turnips, cabbages, and barley: this produce, with the natural resources of the country would greatly encourage an establishment for the education of their children throughout the year: to the support of which the Indians themselves might greatly contribute, and which would be attended with the most beneficial results. In following the track towards the North Pacific Ocean, the climate is much milder than to the East of the mountains, and a vast encouragement would be found in seeking to benefit the natives, from their being strangers to the intoxicating draught of spirituous liquors, in barter for their articles of trade. So little acquainted with the effects of intoxication are some of the Indians in this quarter, that the following circumstance was related to me by an Officer from the mouth of the Columbia. A Chief who had traded but little with Europeans came to the Fort with two of his sons, and two young men of his tribe. During their stay the servants made one of his sons drunk. When the old man saw him foaming at the mouth, uttering the most incoherent expressions, and staggering under the power of the intoxicating draught, he immediately concluded that he was mad, and exclaimed, 'Let him be shot.' It was some time before he could be pacified, which was only effected in a measure by his being assured, that he would see his son recovered from the disorder of his faculties. And when the aged Chief saw him again restored to his right mind, and found him capable of conversing, he manifested the greatest joy.

The Columbia presents every advantage in forming a settlement for the natives or others, particularly so to the south of its entrance to the sea, on the banks of the Willammette River. The soil is excellent; fish and wild fowl are found in abundance, and a good supply of indigenous animals is met with from the praries, or natural meadows. The summer months are very pleasant, but those of winter are frequently rainy, and subject to heavy fogs, which may occasionally render it unhealthy. The Chinnook Indians are six months in villages in the neighbourhood of the Company's Post, Fort George, at the mouth of the Columbia, and afford facilities, with other surrounding tribes for the benevolent attempt of introducing the knowledge of Christianity among them. In their war excursions they adopt a different mode of warfare to that of the Red River Indians, and those towards the Atlantic coast, by openly taking the field against their enemies; and keeping their prisoners alive for slaves. These are numerous among some of the tribes; and many might be obtained, without purchasing them, for religious instruction. In fact there appear to be many points in this vast territory where there is a prospect of establishing well-conducted missions to the great and lasting benefit of the natives. But the object should be pursued upon a regular and persevering system, and while the Missionary needs the active co-operation of the resident Officer in his arduous engagement with the Indians; no idle prejudice should ever prevent his endeavours to civilize and fix them in the cultivation of the soil where it may be effected.

The Russians it appears are affording religious instruction in the establishment of schools for the education of half-caste children, with those of the natives in their Factories on the North-west coast of North America. A gentleman informed me that he saw, at their Establishment at Norfolk Sound, a priest and a schoolmaster, who were teaching the children, and instructing the natives, not as the

Spanish priests do, at Fort St. Francisco, in South America, by taking them by force, and compelling them to go through the forms and ceremonies of *their* religion, but by mild persuasion and conviction; and the report of their success in general is, that a considerable number of savages of the Polar Regions have been converted to Christianity.[8]

May 23.—The Settlers have been very industrious in getting in their seed corn; but the weather has been, and continues to be very cold, with a strong north and north-easterly wind, which has cheeked vegetation; and the woods around us still wear the dark hue of winter. We now take a plentiful supply of sturgeon, and with the return of the feathered tribe we are much annoyed by myriads of blackbirds that destroy a good deal of the new sown grain, as well as when it is ripe for harvest. Multitudes of pigeons also now appear, and unless they are continually shot at, they devour the fruits of husbandry. They fly by millions, and are often seen extending to a vast distance like a cloud; when one flock has passed another succeeds, and we often profit by this kind gift of Providence, by shooting them in their migrations, as excellent food.

There is a general talk among the surrounding tribes of Indians, of going to war against the Sioux nation. A strong band of the Assiniboines are directing their course towards Pembina; and Pigewis, who is by no means a war Chief, is setting off in that direction to join them. Their rage of vengeance towards the Sioux Indians appears to know no bounds; but the scalp of some poor solitary individuals among them will probably terminate the campaign. They cannot keep long together in numerous parties from the want of foresight to provide for their subsistence; and accordingly a little more than a week's absence brought Pigewis back again, with his party, without their having seen an enemy, and in the destitute condition of being without food and moccassins.

CHAPTER VI.

PROGRESS OF INDIAN CHILDREN IN READING. BUILDING FOR DIVINE WORSHIP. LEFT THE COLONY. ARRIVAL AT YORK FORT. DEPARTURE TOR CHURCHILL FACTORY. BEARS. INDIAN HIEROGLYPHICS. ARRIVAL AT CHURCHILL. INTERVIEW WITH ESQUIMAUX. RETURN TO YORK FACTORY. EMBARK FOR ENGLAND. MORAVIAN MISSIONARIES. GREENLAND. ARRIVAL IN THE THAMES.

June 2.—I have been adding two small houses to the Church Mission School, as separate sleeping apartments for the Indian children, who have already made most encouraging progress in reading, and a few of them in writing. In forming this Establishment for their religious education, it is of the greatest importance that they should be gradually inured to the cultivation of the soil, and instructed in the knowledge of agriculture. For this purpose I have allotted a small piece of ground for each child, and divided the different compartments with a wicker frame. We often dig and hoe with our little charge in the sweat of our brow as an example and encouragement for them to labour; and promising them the produce of their own industry, we find that they take great delight in their gardens. Necessity may compel the adult Indian to take up the spade and submit to manual labour, but a child brought up in the love of cultivating a garden will be naturally led to the culture of the field as a means of subsistence: and educated in the principles of Christianity, he will become stationary to partake of the advantages and privileges of civilization. It is through these means of instruction that a change will be gradually effected in the character of the North American Indian, who in his present savage state thinks it beneath the dignity of his independence to till the ground. What we value in property, and all those customs which separate us from them in a state of nature, they think lightly of, while they conclude that our crossing the seas to see their country is more the effect of poverty than of industry. To be a *man*, or what is synonymous with them, to be a great and distinguished character, is to be expert in surprising, torturing, and scalping an enemy; to be capable of enduring severe privations; to make a good hunter, and traverse the woods with geographical accuracy, without any other guide than the tops of the trees, and the course of the sun. These are exploits which, in their estimation, form the hero, and to which the expansion of their mind is confined. Their intellectual powers are very limited, as they enter into no abstruse meditations, or abstract ideas; but what they know in the narrow range of supplying their wants, and combating with their fellow men, they know thoroughly, and are thereby led to consider themselves the standard of excellence. In their fancied superior knowledge they are often heard to remark, when conversing with the European, ""You are almost as clever as an Indian."" They must be educated before they can be led to comprehend the benefits to be received from civilization, or ere a hope can be cherished that their characters will be changed under the mild influence of the Christian religion. Man is as his principles are, and wandering under the influence of those savage-taught habits, in which he has been nurtured, which tend to harden the heart, and narrow all the sources of sympathy, the character of the North American Indian is bold, fierce, unrelenting, sanguinary, and cruel; in fact, a man-devil in war, rejoicing in blood, exulting in the torments he is inflicting on his victim, and then most pleased when his inflictions are most exquisite. We should not be astonished at this character, so repugnant to the sympathies of our nature, nor should we conclude too hastily against him,—he also has his sympathies, and those of no common order. He also loves his parent that begat him, and his child whom he has begotten, with intense affection; he is not without affection from nature; but perverted principle has perverted nature; and as his principle is, so is his practice. Our surprise ceases when we learn that he is trained up in blood, that he is catechized in cruelty, and that he is instructed not in slaughter only, but in torment. Nothing that has life without the pale of his own immediate circle not only does not escape destruction, but is visited with torment also inflicted by his infant hand. If his eye in passing by the lake observes the frog moving in the rushes he instantly seizes his victim, and does not merely destroy it, but often ingeniously torments it by pulling limb from limb. If the duck be but wounded with the gun, his prey is not instantly despatched to spare all future pain, but feather is plucked out after feather, and the hapless creature is tormented on principle. I have frequently witnessed the cruelty with which parents will sometimes amuse their children, by catching young birds or animals, that they may disjoint their limbs to make them struggle in a lingering death. And a child is often seen twisting the neck of a young duck or goose, under the laughing encouragements of the mother for hours together, before it is strangled. At one moment he satisfies the cravings of nature from the breast of his mother, and instantly rewards the boon with a violent blow perhaps on the very breast on which he has been hanging. Nor does the mother dare resent the injury by an appeal to the father. He would at once say that punishment would daunt the spirit of the boy. Hence the Indian never suffers his child to be corrected. We see then the secret spring of his character. He is a murderer by habit, engendered from his earliest age; and the scalping knife and the tomahawk, and the unforgiving pursuit of his own enemy, or his father's enemy, till he has drenched his hands in, and satiated his revenge with his blood, is but the necessary issue of a principle on which his education has been formed. The training of the child forms the maturity of the man.

Our Sunday school is generally attended by nearly fifty scholars, including adults, independent of the Indian children; and the congregation consists upon an average of from one hundred to one hundred and thirty persons. It is a most gratifying sight to see the Colonists, in groups, direct their steps on the Sabbath morning towards the Mission house, at the ringing of the bell, which is now elevated in a spire that is attached to the building. And it is no small satisfaction to have accomplished the wish so feelingly expressed by a deceased officer of the Company. ""*I must confess,* (he observed) *that I am anxious to see the first little Christian church and steeple of wood, slowly rising among the wilds, to hear the sound of the first sabbath bell that has tolled here since the creation.*"" I never witnessed the Establishment but with peculiar feelings of delight, and contemplated it as the dawn of a brighter day in the dark interior of a moral wilderness. The lengthened shadows of the setting sun cast upon the buildings, as I returned from calling upon some of the Settlers a few evenings ago; and the consideration that there was now a landmark of Christianity in this wild waste of heathenism, raised in my mind a pleasing train of thought, with the sanguine hope that this Protestant Establishment might be the means of raising a *spiritual* temple to the Lord, to whom ""the heathen are given as an inheritance, and the utmost parts of the earth as a possession.""

I considered it as a small point gained, to have a public building dedicated to religious purposes, whose spire should catch the eye, both of the wandering natives, and the stationary Colonists. It would have its effect on the population generally. The people of England look with a degree of veneration to the ancient tower and lofty spire of the Establishment; and they are bound in habitual attachment to her constitution, which protects the monument and turf graves of their ancestors. And where the lamp of spiritual Christianity burns but dimly around her altar, it cannot be denied, that even her established rites and outward form have some moral effect on the population at large.

On the 10th, I addressed a crowded congregation, in a farewell discourse, from the pulpit, previous to my leaving the Colony for the Factory: and having administered the sacrament to those who joined cordially with me in prayer, that the Missionary who was on his way to officiate in my absence, might be tenfold, yea a hundred fold, more blessed in his ministry than I had been, I parted with those upon the Church Mission Establishment with tears. It had been a long, and anxious, and arduous scene of labour to me; and my hope was, as about to embark for England, that I might return to the Settlement, and be the means of effecting a better order of things.

The weather was favourable on the morning of our departure; and stepping into the boat the current soon bore us down the river towards Lake Winipeg. As the spire of the church receded from my view, and we passed several of the houses of the Settlers, they hailed me with their cordial wishes for a safe voyage, and expressed a hope of better times for the Colony. Then it was that my heart renewed its supplications to that God,

> —'who is ever present, ever felt,
>
> In the void waste, as in the city full,'

for the welfare of the Settlement, as affording a resting place for numbers, after the toils of the wilderness in the Company's service, where they might dwell, through the divine blessing, in the broad day-light of Christianity; and being bound to the country from having families by native women, might find the protection and advantages of civilized life.

With light favourable winds we soon crossed the Lake and arrived at Norway House, and such is generally the quickness of the passage from this point to York Factory, that in the rapid stream of the rivers, a loaded boat will reach the depot in a few days, which will take three or four weeks to return with excessive toil, from the strength of the opposing current. It appears dangerous to the inexperienced traveller to run the rapids in the passage to the Factory, but it is seldom attended with any serious accident. The men who have charge of the boats are generally experienced steersmen, and it is an interesting sight to see them take the rush of water with their boats, and with cool intrepidity and skill direct the sweep, or steer-oar to their arrival in safety at the bottom of a rapid of almost a perpendicular fall of many feet, or through a torrent of water of a quarter of a mile or more in length. Sometimes, however the boats strike in the violence of their descent, so as to cause a fracture, and hurry the crew to pull ashore to save the cargo from damage. This accident befel us several times in our passage down, but a kind Providence protected us, and we arrived in safety at York Factory.

Immediately on my arrival, I made arrangements for fulfilling my Missionary engagement to visit the Esquimaux at Churchill, the Company's most northern Post on the Bay. It was the advice of Captain Franklin, that I should walk the distance of about one hundred and eighty miles, from York Fort to that Factory, as I might be delayed in a canoe, by the vast quantities of floating ice in the Bay, so as not to meet these Indians in time. I followed this advice, and having engaged one of the Company's servants, with an Indian who was an excellent hunter, we set off on our expedition, on the morning of the 11th of July, accompanied by two Indians, who had come express from Churchill, and were returning thither. It was necessary that we should embark in a boat, to cross the North River; and in rowing round the Point of Marsh, we perceived a brightness in the northern horizon, like that reflected from ice, usually called the *blink*, and which led us to suppose that vast fields of it were floating along the coast in the direction that we were going. It happened to be low water when we crossed the mouth of the river, so that the boat could not approach nearer than about a mile from the shore, which obliged us to walk this distance through the mud and water, to the place where we made our encampment for the night, and where the mosquitoes inflicted their torments upon us. We were dreadfully annoyed by them, from the swampy country we had to traverse, and I was glad to start with the dawn of the following morning, from a spot where they literally blackened a small canvass tent that was pitched, and hovered around us in clouds so as to render life itself burdensome. The day, however, afforded us very little relief, while walking, nearly ancle deep in water, through the marshes; and such was their torture upon the poor animals, that we frequently saw the deer coming out of the woods, apparently almost blinded and distracted with their numbers, to rush into the water on the shore for relief. This gave an opportunity to the hunter to kill two of them in the course of the afternoon, so that we had plenty of venison, and a good supply of wild fowl, which he had shot for our evening repast. We started at sunrise the next morning, after having had but little sleep, as I had been wrapped in my blanket almost to suffocation, to escape in a degree the misery of our unceasing torment. Towards noon, we had much better walking than we had before met with, and were relieved from the mosquitoes by a change of wind blowing cold from off the ice, which was now seen from the horizon to the shores of the bay. The relief to us was like a cessation from an agony of pain; and as the hunter had just killed another deer, and the wild fowl flew around us in abundance, we pitched the tent, and halted for several hours, and refreshed ourselves with sleep, after the irritation and almost sleepless nights that we had endured. We were on the march again at five o'clock; and after we had forded Stoney River, we came upon the track of a polar bear. The Indian hunter was very keen in his desire to fall in with it, and I lamented that I had not an opportunity of seeing him engage the ferocious animal, which seemed to have taken a survey of the party, and to have gone into the wood a short distance from us. The bears are now coming off the ice in the Bay, on which they have been for several months past, to live upon seals, which they catch as they lie sleeping by the sides of the holes in the drift ice, when it dissolves or is driven far from shore. They seek their food among the sea-weed and every trash that is washed up along the coast, or go upon the rocks, or to the woods, for berries, during the summer months. Savage, however, as this animal is, it is not so much dreaded by the Indians as the grizzly bear, which is more ferocious and forward in his attack. These are found towards the Rocky Mountains, and none but very expert hunters like to attack them. A gentleman who was travelling to a distance on the plains to the West of the Red River Colony, told me of a narrow escape he once had, with his servant boy, in meeting a grizzly bear. They were riding slowly along, near the close of the day, when they espied the animal coming from the verge of a wood in the direction towards them. They immediately quickened the pace of their horses, but being jaded with the day's journey, the bear was soon seen to gain upon them. In this emergency, he hit upon an expedient, which was probably the means of saving their lives. He took the boy, who was screaming with terror, behind him, and abandoned the horse that he rode. When the ferocious animal came up to it, the gentleman, who stopped at some distance, expected to see the bear rend it immediately with his paws; but to his surprise, after having walked round and smelt at the horse, as it stood motionless with fear, the bear returned to the wood, and the horse was afterwards recovered without injury.

The morning of the 14th was very cold, from the wind blowing off the ice in the Bay; and when we stopped to breakfast, I was obliged to put a blanket over my shoulders, as I stood by the fire, for warmth. The comfortable sensation however was, that we were free from the annoyance and misery of the mosquitoes; cold, hunger, and thirst, are not to be compared with the incessant suffering which they inflict. We waded knee-deep through Owl River, in the afternoon of the 15th. The weather was cold, and nothing was to be seen in the Bay but floating ice. It was rather late before we pitched the tent, and we met with some difficulty in collecting a sufficient quantity of drift wood on the shore, to kindle a fire large enough to boil the kettle, and cook the wild fowl that we had shot. The next day we forded Broad River, on the banks of which we saw several dens, which the bears had scratched for shelter: and seeing the smoke of an Indian tent at some distance before us, in the direction we were going, we quickened our step, and reached it before we stopped to breakfast. We found the whole family clothed in deerskins, and upon a hunting excursion from Churchill. The Indian, or rather a half-breed, was very communicative, and told me that though he was leading an Indian life, his father was formerly a master at one of the Company's Posts, and proposed accompanying our party to the Factory. He had two sons, he said, who were gone in the pursuit of a deer; and, on quitting the encampment to travel with us, he would leave some signs for them to follow us on their return. They were the following, and drawn upon a broad piece of wood, which he prepared with an axe.

1. To intimate that the family was gone forward.
2. That there was a Chief of the party.
3. That he was accompanied by a European servant.
4. And also by an Indian.
5. That there were two Indians in company.
6. That they should follow.

It is a common custom with the Indians to paint hieroglyphic characters on dressed buffaloe skins or robes; and a variety of figures are drawn on many of those which they barter at the Company's Posts. In the representation of a victory achieved over an enemy, the picture of the Chief is given, with the mark of his nation, and those of the warriors who accompanied him. A number of little images point out how many prisoners were taken; while so many human figures without heads shew the number who were slain. Such are the expressive signs of a barbarous people, in recording their war exploits, and communicating information without the knowledge of letters and the art of printing.

We proceeded, after the wife had put some kettles upon the back of a miserable looking dog, and had taken her accustomed burden, the tent with other articles, on her own. The little ones were also severally laden with a knapsack, and the whole had the appearance of a camp of gypsies moving through the country.

The 17th. Before we struck our tents this morning, the signs which the old man left upon the piece of wood yesterday, brought his two sons, whom he had left hunting, and who had walked nearly the whole of the night to overtake us. We had now no provisions but what we shot on our journey, and the addition to our party made every one active in the pursuit of game as it appeared. The next day we passed Cape Churchill, and came to a tent of Chipewyan or Northern Indians. The question was not asked if we were hungry, but immediately on our arrival the women were busily employed in cooking venison for us; and the men proposed to go with us to Churchill. As soon as we had finished eating, the tent was struck, and the whole party proceeded, with the old man ahead, with a long staff in his hand, followed by his five sons and two daughters, and the rest of us in the train, which suggested to my mind the patriarchal mode of travelling. The 19th, our progress was slow, from being again annoyed with mosquitoes, in a bad track, through a wet swampy ground. As soon as we had passed the beacon, which was erected as a landmark to the shipping that formerly sailed to Churchill, as the Company's principal depôt, before its destruction by Pérouse, two of the Indians left us, to take a circuit through some islands by the sea, to hunt for provision. We pitched our tents early, in expectation that they would join us, but we saw nothing of them that evening. It is customary, as we were then travelling, to take only one blanket, in which you roll yourself for the night, without undressing. On laying down, upon a few willow twigs, I soon afterwards felt so extremely cold, from the wind blowing strong off a large field of ice drifted on the shore, that I was obliged to call the servant to take down the tent, and wrap it round me, before I could get any sleep. The sudden variation of the weather, however, gave me no cold, nor did it interrupt a good appetite, which the traveller in these regions usually enjoys.

Had we not been delayed by the absence of the Indians a hunting we might have reached the Factory to-day, the 20th. They came in from their excursion at the time we were taking our breakfast, but without much success. They had killed an Arctic fox that supplied them with a meal, and a few ducks which they brought to our encampment, among which was the Eider duck, so remarkable for the beautiful softness of its down. In the evening one of the Chipewyan

Indians, sent me some dried venison; and the next morning early we arrived at Churchill. The Esquimaux, Augustus, who accompanied Captain Franklin to the shores of the Polar Sea, came out to meet us, and expressed much delight at my coming to see his tribe, who were expected to arrive at the Factory every day. He had not seen his countrymen since he acted as one of the guides in that arduous expedition, and intended to return with them to his wife and children, laden with presents and rewards for his tried and faithful services.

July 25.—The servants, with the Officers, assembled for divine service, and laborious as is the office of a Missionary, I felt delighted with its engagements; and thought it a high privilege to *visit even* the wild inhabitants of the rocks with the *simple design* of extending the Redeemer's kingdom among them; and that in a remote quarter of the globe, where probably no Protestant Minister had ever placed his foot before. The next day a northern Indian leader, came to the Fort with his family; and upon making known to him the object of my journey to meet the Esquimaux, he cheerfully promised to give up one of his boys, a lively active little fellow, to be educated at the Native School Establishment at the Red River. He appeared very desirous of having his boy taught more than the Indians knew; and assisted me in obtaining an orphan boy from a widow woman, who was in a tent at a short distance, to accompany his son. I told him that they must go a long way, (Churchill being about a thousand miles distant from the Colony) but that they would be taken great care of. He made no objection, but said that they should go, and might return when they had learnt enough. This was a striking instance of the confidence of an Indian, and confirmed the opinion that they would part with their children to those in whom they thought they could justly confide, and to whose kind tuition they were persuaded they could safely entrust them. The Company's boats were going to York Factory, and would take them there; where, on my return, I expected to meet my successor as a Minister to the Settlement, on his arrival from England by the ship; and who would take them under his care in continuing the voyage to the school. ""Religion, (says Hearne) has not as yet began to dawn among the Northern Indians; for, though their conjurors do indeed sing songs and make long speeches to some beasts and birds of prey, as also to imaginary beings, which they say assist them in performing cures on the sick, yet they, as well as their credulous neighbours, are utterly destitute of every idea of practical religion.""

The Company's present Establishment is about five miles up the river, from the point of rock at its entrance where the ruins of the old Factory are seen; which was the point Hearne started from on his journey to the Coppermine River, in the year 1770; and which was blown up by Pèrouse about the year 1784. It appears to have been strongly fortified, and from its situation must have been capable of making a formidable resistance to an enemy; and it can never cease to be a matter of surprise that it should have been surrendered without firing a shot. The walls and bastions are still remaining, which are strewed with a considerable number of cannon, spiked, and of a large calibre. Augustus used to visit this point every morning, in anxious expectation that his countrymen would arrive by the way of the coast, in their seal skin canoes. One day he returned to the Factory evidently much agitated; and upon inquiry I found that there was an Esquimaux family in a tent by the shore, under one of the rocks, one of whom had greatly alarmed him with the information, that soon after he left his tribe with Junius, (who is supposed to have perished as a guide in the Arctic Expedition,) one of Junius's brothers took his wife, and thinking that Augustus was displeased with him, and that he possessed the art of conjuring, had determined upon his death, and that this superstitious notion had so preyed upon his spirits as to terminate his existence. This circumstance, he added, had led a surviving brother to threaten revenge, and supposing that he might come to the Factory with the Esquimaux who were expected, he advised him to be on his guard. The next day, July the 29th, Augustus returned to the point of rock on the look out, but not without having first requested a brace of pistols, loaded his musket, and fixed his bayonet, yet nothing was seen of his countrymen. The next morning I accompanied him to the Esquimaux tent, with an interpreter, under the idea that I might obtain some interesting information; and was much pleased to find the family living in the apparent exercise of social affection. The Esquimaux treated his wife with kindness; she was seated in the circle who were smoking the pipe, and there was a constant smile upon her countenance, so opposite to that oppressed dejected look of the Indian women in general. I asked the Esquimaux of his country: he said it was good, though there was plenty of cold and snow; but that there was plenty of musk oxen and deer; and the corpulency of the party suggested the idea that there was seldom a want of food amongst them. I told him that mine was better, as growing what made the biscuit, of which they were very fond, and that there was much less cold, and that we saw the water much longer than they did. Observing that the woman was tattooed, I asked him when these marks were made, on the chin, particularly, and on the hands. His reply was, when the girls were marriageable, and espoused to their husbands; who had generally but one wife, though good hunters had sometimes two. Wishing to know whether they ever abandoned the aged and the infirm to perish like the Northern Indians, he said, never; assuring me that they always dragged them on sledges with them in winter to the different points where they had laid up provisions in the autumn, 'en cache;' and that they took them in their canoes in summer till they died. Knowing that some Indians west of the rocky mountains burn their dead, I asked him if this custom prevailed with the Esquimaux, he said, no; and that they always buried theirs. The name of this Esquimaux was *Achshannook*, and as Augustus could write a little, which he had been taught during the time he was with the expedition, I gave him my pencil, that the other might see what I wished to teach the Esquimaux children, as well as to read white man's book, which told us true of the Great Spirit, whom the Esquimaux did not know, and how they were to live and die happy. The woman immediately caught up her little girl about five years of age, and holding her towards me manifested the greatest delight, with Achshannook, at the wish I had expressed of having the Esquimaux children taught to write and read the book. They often pointed in the direction the others were coming, and gave me to understand that they would soon arrive. We returned to the Fort, and walking by the side of the river we saw numbers of white whales which frequent it at this season of the year, and many of which are harpooned from a boat that is employed, and usually carries three or four of the Company's servants. The harpooner killed one to-day, which measured fourteen feet long, and eight in girth, and weighed it was supposed a ton weight. The blubber is boiled at the Fort, and the oil sent to England as an article of the Company's trade. When the Esquimaux visit us from the tent, they generally go to the spot where the carcases of the whales are left to rot after the blubber is taken, and carry away a part, but generally from the fin or the tail; they have been known, however, to take the maggots from the putrid carcase, and to boil them with train oil as a rich repast. They are extremely filthy in their mode of living. The Esquimaux who was engaged at the Fort as an interpreter, used to eat the fish raw as he took them out of the net, and devour the head and entrails of those that were cooked by the Company's servants. And it is their constant custom, when their noses bleed by any accident to lick their blood into their mouths and swallow it.

Though the beaver, which furnishes the staple fur of the country, is not common in this immediate neighbourhood, an Indian was successful enough to kill one at a short distance down the river, which he brought to the Fort. It was roasted for dinner, and proved of excellent flavour, though I could not agree that the tail, which was served up in a separate dish, was of that superior taste it is generally considered to be. The sagacity of this animal has often been described; and I have frequently been surprised at the singular construction of their houses, the care with which they lay up their provision of wood, and the mode in which they dam up the water near their habitations. They cut with their teeth sticks of a considerable size, and when larger than they are able to drag, they contrive to fell them on the bank, so that they may fall and float down the stream to the place where they design to make the dam; and then entwine them with willow twigs, which they plaster with mud, so as effectually to obtain a head of water.

We met again on the Sabbath for divine worship on both parts of the day, as we had done on the previous Sunday. As the Esquimaux did not make their appearance, we began to think that the ice in the Bay might have prevented their coming to the Factory. We were relieved from our doubts however, on the 2nd of August, by Augustus running to the Fort with the information that his countrymen were seen coming along in their canoes. He waited till he ascertained that Junius's brother, who was said to have threatened his life, was not of the party, and then went to meet them. Some of them came over the rocks with the canoes upon their heads, as being a much nearer way to the Company's Post from the spot where they left the Bay, than following the course of the river. Their number, with a small party that came soon afterwards, was forty-two men, who brought with them a considerable quantity of the Arctic fox skins, musk-ox, and deer skins, with those of the wolf and wolverine, together with sea-horse teeth, and the horn of a sea-unicorn about six feet long for barter at the Company's Post. In appearance they strongly resembled each other, and were all clothed with deerskin jackets and lower garments of far larger than usually Dutch size, made of the same material. Their stature was low, like that of the wife of the Esquimaux at the tent who was not five feet in height. They were all very broad set, with remarkably small eyes, low foreheads, and of a very fine bronze complexion. A few of the men however were nearly six feet in stature, and of a strong robust make. As soon as they had bartered the articles which they brought with them for those they requested in return, which were guns, ammunition, beads, and blankets principally, they were informed that I had travelled a long way to see them, and to have some talk with them.

The next day, they gathered round me, and with Augustus and an interpreter, I was enabled to make the object of my visit to them well understood. I told them that I came very far across the great lake, because I loved the Esquimaux; that there were very many in my country who loved them also, and would be pleased to hear that I had seen them. I spoke true. I did not come to their country, thinking it was better than mine, nor to make house and trade with them, but to enquire, and they must speak true, if they would like white man to make house and live amongst them, to teach their children white man's knowledge, and of the Great and Good Spirit who made the world. The sun was then shining in his glory, and the scenery in the full tide of the water before us was striking and beautiful; when I asked them, if they knew who made the heavens, the waters, and the earth, and all things that surrounded us, so pleasing to our sight? their reply was, 'We do not know whether the Person who made these things is dead or alive.' On assuring them that I knew, and that it was my real wish that they and their children should know also the Divine Being, who was the Creator of all things; and on repeating the question, whether they wished that white man should come and give them this knowledge, they all simultaneously expressed a great desire that he should, laughing and shouting, ""heigh! heigh! augh! augh!"" One of them afterwards gave me a map of the coast which they traversed, including Chesterfield Inlet, and which he drew with a pencil that I lent him, with great accuracy, pointing out to me the particular rivers where the women speared salmon in the rapids in summer, while the men were employed in killing the deer, as they crossed in the water some points of the Inlet; or were hunting on the coast, catching seals. Being provident, and not so regardless of the morrow as the Indians in general, they lay up provisions at these different places for the winter, and probably seldom suffer from want of food; nor are they long in summer without their favourite dish of the flesh and fat of the seal, mixed with train oil as a sauce, which they prefer to salmon; and when not mixed with their food, they drink the oil as a cordial.

The Esquimaux often surrounded me in groups, during their stay at the Factory, and cordially shaking hands, were fond of saying, that the Northern Indians, or Chipewyans, sprang from dogs, but that they were formerly as white men. I encouraged them in the idea that we were originally of the same parents, but that they being scattered, we knew now a great deal more than they did, and therefore came to see if it were possible to teach their children our knowledge, for their happiness, and also themselves, if it were their desire. They appeared to be quite overjoyed at this conversation, and laughed heartily, shouting, ""Heigh! heigh!"" saying, (as the interpreter expressed it,) ""We want to know the Grand God.""

I told them that there were stones on the edge of the water, in their country, and that with a little wood, a house might be made like what they saw at the Fort. Should I, or any other person, ever come from across the great lake, to build this house, where their children might live, and be taught what I had told them; I asked if they would assist to bring the stones, and help to raise the building. They signified their willingness by shouting again in their usual manner. I mentioned the above circumstance, as conceiving it to be practicable and advisable, from the best information I could obtain, that the first attempt to form an establishment on the shores of the Bay, to educate the children of the Esquimaux, should be made at Knapp's Bay, or, as called by the Esquimaux, Aughlinatook. Augustus's tribe traverse this part of the coast, which is about two hundred miles north of Churchill; from whence the frame of the building and some dry provisions in casks might be taken in boats, to maintain the party, at first making the settlement, independent of the common resources of the country, and of the Esquimaux; and a communication kept up with the Company's Post, which might easily be done, both in summer and winter. It is said that the word, difficulty, is not known in the English Military dictionary, and surely ought not to be found in that of the Missionary; and a mission undertaken to the Esquimaux, upon the plan suggested, conducted with prudence, intrepedity, and perseverance, can leave little doubt as to its ultimate success. They tied knots upon a sinew thread, tieing a knot for each child as it was named, to inform me, at my request, of the number of children they had belonging to their tribe, and which they would bring to the school for instruction. The number on the sinew thread was sixty-two boys and sixty-four girls. Whenever I spoke to them about provisions, they uniformly said that they would bring plenty; but should the establishment be made, a small number of children would at first of course be taken, and increased in proportion as the resources of the country, and the supplies afforded by the Esquimaux towards the support of their children, were pretty accurately ascertained. It is true that they live in a country, as those do on the Labrador coast, of hopeless barrenness, and endure almost a perpetual winter's blast; but the success of the faithful devoted Moravian Missionaries, on the coast of Labrador, and on that of Greenland, in their labours, privations, and perseverance, to impart the knowledge of Christianity, which has been blessed of God to the salvation of the Esquimaux, holds out every encouragement to the intrepid Missionary, in his attempts to benefit, with Christian instruction, those on the shores of Hudson's Bay.

'Cold is the clime, the winds are bleak,

And wastes of trackless snow,

Ye friends of our incarnate God!

Obscure the paths ye go.

'But hearts more cold, and lusts more fierce,

And wider wastes of sin,
Ye Preachers of redeeming love!
Obscure the soul within.
'Yet go: and though both poles combine,
To freeze the sinner's soul,
The sinner's soul shall yield to grace,
For grace can melt the pole.
'Then blow ye winds, and roll ye waves,
Your task assigned perform:
The God of grace is nature's God,
And rides upon the storm.
'Nature and Providence obey
The dictates of his grace;
Go! for each drop subserves his cause
Each atom has its place.'

A few of the Esquimaux who came to the Fort, were from Chesterfield Inlet, and proposed to return, before the other party left us for Knapp's Bay. Before they started, Augustus was very desirous that I should see his countrymen conjure; and bringing a blanket and a large knife, he assured me that one of them would swallow the knife, and not die; or fire a ball through his body, leaning upon a gun, without being injured. I understood that he was to perform this jugglery with the blanket round him, which I objected to, if I saw it; but told him that I had great objections to such deceptions and art, by which they imposed on each other; and observed, that if his countrymen could really conjure, they should conjure the whales to the shore, which were then sporting in the river before us. He was not pleased, however, with my refusal, and it was with difficulty that I prevented the exhibition. When the party left us, they encircled me, and said that they would tell all of their tribe what had been mentioned about teaching the Esquimaux children white man's knowledge of the Great Spirit. They informed me that a great many of the Esquimaux meet in summer about Chesterfield Inlet; that some come down from the great lake to the north, and that they had met some, who had seen two very large canoes when there was no ice; and when one of these canoes stood in towards the shore where they were, they were so alarmed as to run off over the rocks, and that they did not return till the big canoes were out of sight towards where the sun rises. This information led me to suppose that they were the Discovery Ships, under the command of Captain Parry; and to conjecture that the ice had been a barrier to his progress in search of a North-West Passage, and that he was returning down the Bay to England. The object of the Esquimaux in meeting from different tribes at Chesterfield Inlet every year, is to barter with those principally who trade at Churchill Factory, and also with some Northern Indians, who exchange what European articles they may have for fish-hooks made of bone, and sinew lines, and skins. I then shook hands with them, and gave to each individual a clasp-knife, some tobacco, and a few beads, to take with them to their wives, with which they were much pleased, telling me, not to be afraid to come to their country, as Esquimaux would treat me well.

August 7.—When the remaining party returned to Knapp's Bay, it was proposed by the Master of the Company's Posts, that they should stop for a few days at Seal River, about fifty miles north of Churchill, and spear white whales for the blubber. This they readily assented to, and the day after they started, I accompanied the officer in a boat to the point where they were to be employed. We pitched our tents near the place where they rested at night, and were much amused at their dexterity in spearing a number of whales on the following day. In the course of two days they harpooned about forty, so numerous were these animals in the Bay at the mouth of the river. These Esquimaux were not unacquainted with habits of cleanliness, for they were no sooner ashore from spearing whales, than they changed their dirty skin dress for one of a newer and cleaner character; and in seating themselves in a circle, around a small fire they had made, I observed that while they boiled the skin of the whale, and some partook of it, others were eating the tail and the fin in a raw state. I never knew natives more orderly and less troublesome; we were in their power, but so far from annoying us, they never even came to our tents, importuning for tobacco and other articles, as is generally the case with Indians when near their own encampment.

Wishing to talk with them again on the subject of teaching their children, I invited to my tent seven of the oldest men among them; and repeated to them the questions which I had put to the whole of them before. They expressed the same feelings in favour of instruction, and a hope that I was not afraid to come to their country, promising, when white man came, not to steal from him, a vice which they are sometimes guilty of at the Factory. I found that they believed in a future state; and acknowledged that there was a bad Spirit, who made them suffer, and to whom they prayed that he would not hurt them. They thought that when a bad man died, the bad Spirit took him, and put him in a hole under ground, where there was always fire, but this idea they might have got from their intercourse with Europeans at the Fort: and when a good man died, they believed that the moon took him up, where he lived as he had done below, only that he had always plenty to enjoy, and less paddling to do. In parting with these Indians, as with the others who returned to Chesterfield Inlet, I gave to each individual a clasp knife, some tobacco, and a few beads to take to their wives; and my prayer to God was, that some effectual step might be taken to communicate to these heathen, that knowledge which they appeared desirous of receiving, and which would ameliorate their condition through a scriptural hope of a future life.

We returned to the Factory, along a coast the most dangerous to navigate that can possibly be conceived, from fragments of rocks being studded in the water for miles from the shore, and which are only visible at the reflux of the tide. The safest course to take is to run out to sea, and sail along out of sight of land; but this is hazardous in an open boat, if the weather be stormy, or the water is much ruffled by the wind. The Company lost a boat's crew last fall, as they were returning to Churchill, from one of the points of rock where they had been to collect geese, which the Indians had shot, and which are salted as part of the winter supply of provisions at the Establishment. At first it was supposed that the boat had been driven out to sea, and all had perished in a most painful manner;

but during our stay, an Indian came to the Fort, to inform the officer that the empty boat was lying on the beach, about six or seven miles to the south of Churchill River. He immediately sent men to the spot, and to search along the coast for some remains at least of the bodies of the crew, but not the least appearance of them could be found. The boat filled and went down, with the sail set and fastened to the mast, which was the state in which it was found; but whether she struck upon the point of a sunken rock, or swamped at the conflux of the waters off the mouth of the river at the return of the tide, not a man survived to tell the melancholy tale.

The 10th.—I began to make preparations for my return to York Factory, in the supply of ammunition and a couple of days' provisions for our journey. As every thing we took was borne on the back of the men, we deemed this sufficient, with the supply we were likely to obtain in our walk through a country which at this season of the year generally abounds with wildfowl. It was painful to see several Indian women in an infirm state of health and lame, continually begging for a little oatmeal, or picking *tripe de roche* for a subsistence, being unable to follow the tribe they belonged to; and, upon inquiry, I found that it was a common custom among the Chipewyans, to leave the aged, the infirm, and the sick, when supposed incapable of recovery, to perish for want! and that one-half of the aged probably die in this miserable condition! The common feelings of humanity suggest the question,—Could not some establishment be formed, as a hospital for the reception of a certain number at least of the aged and infirm; towards the maintenance of which, the Indians themselves, in bringing their relations, might be induced to contribute, were it only the tenth skin from the produce of their hunting? If this establishment could not be formed near the coast, might not one be made as an experiment on the borders of their country in the Athabasca? where grain and Indian corn might be raised towards its support. The subject at least challenges inquiry, and is fraught with deep interest, as calling forth the best feelings of benevolence; for a more deplorable situation in existence cannot be conceived, than for persons to be deserted in afflictive old age, suffering infirmity, and left at the last stage of life to expire in want, when, of all other periods in our mortal career, we most need attention, and sympathy, and kindness.

These Indians have a singular custom of wrestling for any woman to whom they are attached; and she has to witness the contest, which consists in hauling each other about by the hair of the head, without kicking or striking, till the strongest party carries her off as his prize. And instead of stabbing one another in their quarrels, as is frequently the case with the Southern Indians, these generally decide them by wrestling. They may permit a weak man, if he be a good hunter, to keep the object of his choice; but otherwise he is obliged to yield his wife to a stronger man, who may think her worth his notice. This barbarous custom I should suppose prevails among the Esquimaux who visit Churchill Factory, as they pointed out to me, at the time I saw them, a weakly looking man, who they said had his wife taken from him by another of superior strength. They shewed me also how they decided their quarrels, by each party alternately bending the body in a horizontal position, and receiving from each other a blow of the fist on the temple or side of the face.

On the 12th, we left Churchill Factory, and in our track killed plenty of wild-fowl, and were again tortured with the mosquitoes, till after the second day's march, when we waded through a low swampy ground, frequently half-leg deep in water, to some dry ridges of land. The wind blew again off the ice in the bay, which enabled us to walk without much annoyance; and in our progress, we often passed large holes, which the bears had scratched in these ridges to lie in, and which, from the impression of their paws on the sand, several had recently left. On the 17th, we came to a tent of Indians, who were encamped on the shore, for the purpose of killing them, in the front of which was the head of one that they had lately shot, stuck upon some painted sticks, in expression of some superstitious notions respecting the animal. They have a great dread of bears, and are very fond of wearing their claws round their necks, ornamented as a necklace, under the idea that they shall be preserved from their ferocious attacks. A short time before I left the Red River Colony, a Saulteaux Indian came to my residence with a necklace strung with some large claws; and prevailing upon him to part with it for some tobacco, he addressed it in a very grave speech, when he took it from his neck, and laid it for me on the table, in language to the following effect:—""My grandfather! you and I have been together some time—we must now part. Go to that Chief; and in leaving me, be not angry, but let me kill buffaloe when I am hungry, and another bear when I meet with it, and then I will make another necklace of the claws."" I smiled at this address, when, looking at me very seriously, he said, ""If you offend the bear,"" (I supposed he meant the spirit of the bear, whose claws he had given me,) ""the bears will be sure to eat you.""

On the 18th, some Indians whom we met, told us that they had heard the great guns of the ship, on her arrival from England, though they had not seen her at anchor. The next day convinced us of the fact; and we reached York Factory early the following morning, after having walked on our return from Churchill, the supposed distance of one hundred and eighty miles, through a trackless path in swamps and long grass, in less than seven days.

Here I had the happiness of meeting the Rev. Mr. Jones, arrived by the ship, on his way to the Red River Settlement, my fellow-labourer in that situation; to whom I committed the two Chipewyan Indian boys. After a few days, he proceeded with his little charge to his destination. And may God, whom we serve in the gospel of his Son, abundantly bless his exertions, on entering upon a field of anxious and laborious toil, which I have just left, to visit the land of my nativity and affection, after an absence of more than three years.

York Factory, as the principal depôt, is rapidly improving in appearance, and in the extent of its buildings. A number of the chief Factors and Traders meet here every summer, and a council is held for the management of the *Northern Factory*; while another is also annually held at Moose, in St. James's Bay, for the direction of the *Southern Factory*. This division of the Company's territory, comprises the whole of the country, from the furthest known point to the north to the boundary line of the United States, and from the waters of the Pacific to those of the Atlantic. In carrying into effect the moral improvement of the country, which has long been contemplated, it would be very desirable that schools should be established at the Company's chief depôts; where it is presumed provisions might be obtained, for the support at least of a limited number of the half-caste children. And the most beneficial results might follow the regular performance of divine worship on the Sabbath, by a Clergyman, throughout the summer months at least, in a building erected and appropriated as a chapel. These are arrangements, which every benevolent mind, truly desirous of promoting the best interests of the country, where the progress of moral and religious instruction would be but slow, would rejoice to see practically entered upon.

It may be stated with pleasure that directions have been given to lessen the quantity of spirituous liquors in barter with the natives. The baneful effects of such a medium of trade have long been deplored by all who have regarded the amelioration of their state, and sought to improve their wandering condition. Cruelty, disease, and premature decay have for centuries past been generated wherever Europeans have introduced the exchange of ardent spirits with the Indians. No act therefore can be more beneficial and humane than that of gradually altering a system which is at once so prejudicial to the native, and injurious to the morals of the trader. It is to be hoped that the benevolent intentions of the Honourable Committee will be carried into full effect, together with the resolutions passed in council at York Factory, July 1823, for the purpose of improving the moral state, both of the Indians and of the European inhabitants of the Company's territory; an event highly interesting to every friend of humanity and religion.

Sept. 10.—We embarked on board the ship Prince of Wales on her return to England, and left the anchorage next day with a favourable wind. The weather being moderate, on Sunday the 14th we enjoyed the privilege of having two full services.

The 16th.—The wind continues light and favourable, and I have been much interested in reading Mr. Wilberforce's pamphlet, entitled, ""An Appeal in behalf of the Negro Slaves."" When will men regard each other as brethren, connected by the common ties of humanity, and as generally responsible to God, the Judge of all.

Sunday, 21st.—When off Cape Charles at the entrance of Hudson's straits, the Thermometer I observed was as low as 24°#176;; and the land as we passed along was covered with snow. The prospect was most chilling and dreary. Though it blew fresh, there was not however a heavy swell of the sea, which gave us the opportunity of having divine service both morning and afternoon. I felt humbled in going through the Ministerial duties of the day; and the experience of my heart imposes on me the obligation of labouring more and more after humiliation. What a consolation is it to *know* that we are saved by hope, even in Him, who sitteth upon the circle of the heavens, directing the course of the elements—who commandeth the waters and they obey Him.

On the 23d we encountered a heavy gale of wind, with a short and angry sea, insomuch that the ship was covered with waves, and all on board were reeling to and fro, and staggering like a drunken man. Towards evening it blew a hurricane; the heavens were black with tempest, and all around us appeared awfully dangerous. Self-examination is at all times profitable and incumbent on the Christian, but when dangers press around him in a tumultuous scene of waters, it is peculiarly consolatory for him to find upon examination, that the sheet anchor of his hope is well grounded; and that he has laboured in the cause of his divine Lord with a conscious integrity, though with a conscious imperfection of character. It was *well* said by the wife of a Missionary, in her last moments, when it was observed to her that she was dying a sacrifice in the cause of missions, ""*I would rather* (said she) *die a penitent sinner at the cross of Christ.*"" Every day, in the smooth unruffled calm of life, or on the tempestuous ocean of its existence, would I *feel* the sentiment so expressive of the Christian's security, and simple reliance upon the omnipotent arm of the Saviour, as uttered by St. Peter, when ready to sink amidst the threatening waves, ""Lord save us, we perish.""

During the 25th we were becalmed off the Upper Savage Islands, amidst several large icebergs, some of which were stranded on the shore, and would receive the accumulation of another winter's fall of snow, from not being driven out of the Straits into the Atlantic Ocean, where they are dissolved. The winter was again setting in with a cold frosty air, and frequent snow storms. The next morning the wind freshened, and on the 27th, when we were off Saddle Back, we experienced another heavy gale of wind, which was so violent about eight o'clock in the evening, that it broke the mizen top sail yard, while nine of the sailors were furling the sail. Providentially the broken part of the yard slung with the ropes, or every soul must inevitably have perished, from the violent rolling of the ship. A more rough and stormy night could not well be experienced, with the aggravated danger of sailing among a number of large isles of floating ice; the running foul of one of which would be immediate destruction, as upon a rock.

The next day the wind moderated, and was favourable, but from the rolling of the ship I could only read the morning and evening prayers, and that with some difficulty, when we met for divine worship. In the evening we approached Resolution Island, and the waters of the Atlantic opened to us with the encouraging prospect of having more sea room to encounter any storms that we might afterwards meet with. As we left the barren rugged shores of the Straits, and the chain of rocks terminating in ragged points on the coast of Labrador, there was a general spirit of congratulation; and the prospect of crossing the great Western Ocean in safety raised in my mind the ascription of praise uttered by the Psalmist, ""Praise the Lord, O my soul, and forget not all his benefits.""

Oct. 4.—We were off Cape Farewell, South Greenland, with strong gales of wind. This point called to my mind the labours of the Moravian Missionaries who had formed several settlements, the most southern of which I believe is Lichterau, among the Greenlanders, under far greater difficulties, than are likely to assail the Missionary, in his attempt to form an establishment for the instruction of the same race of people in the principles of divine truth on the shores of Hudson's Bay, with the aid and co-operation of the Hudson's Bay Company. These pious, simple, devoted Missionaries, have proved that missions to the heathen on the most inhospitable and barren shores are not visionary schemes, but succeed effectually under the blessing of heaven to the conversion of the natives; and they have established the principle, that wherever the waters roll, and however barren the rock on which man is to be found, there man may be benefitted with the saving knowledge and blessings of Christianity. The account given of the first Missionaries of the United Brethren, whose entrance upon the inhospitable and icy coasts of Greenland was in 1733, among whom was that eminent servant of the mission, Matthew Stach, is truly interesting. Leaving Hernnhutt, they first proceeded to the Danish capital, as Greenland was under that government, to obtain the sanction of the King, in their intended mission. Their first audience with the Chamberlain was not a little discouraging, but being convinced, by a closer acquaintance of the solidity of their faith, and the rectitude of their intentions, this Minister became their firm friend, and willingly presented their memorial to the King, who was pleased to approve of their design, and wrote a letter with his own hand, recommending them to the notice of the Danish Missionary, Egede, who had undertaken a mission to Greenland in 1721, but had hitherto accomplished very little in the way of success, notwithstanding his indefatigable exertions.

The Chamberlain also introduced them to several persons distinguished by rank and piety, who liberally contributed toward the expense of their voyage and intended settlement. Being asked one day by his Excellency, how they proposed to maintain themselves in Greenland, they answered, that they depended on the labour of their own hands and God's blessing; and that not to be burdensome to any one, they would build themselves a house and cultivate the ground. It being objected that they would find no wood to build with, as the country presented little but a face of barren rock. ""Then,"" replied they in a true Missionary spirit, ""we will dig into the earth and lodge there."" ""No,"" said the Minister, ""to that necessity you shall not be reduced; you shall take timber with you for building a house; accept of these fifty dollars for that purpose."" With this and other donations, they purchased poles, planks and laths; instruments for agriculture, and carpenter's work, together with several sorts of seeds and roots, with provisions. Thus equipped, says Crantz, they took an affectionate leave of the Court where they had been so hospitably entertained, and embarked on the 10th of April, on board the King's ship, Caritas, Capt. Hildebrand. The congregation at Hernhutt had already adopted the custom of annually compiling a collection of scripture texts for every day in the year, each illustrated or applied by a short verse from some hymn. This text was called the ""daily word,"" it supplied a profitable subject for private meditation, and a theme for the public discourses. The daily word on the morning of their embarkation on a mission which so often appeared to baffle all hope, was, '*Faith is the substance of things hoped for, the evidence of things not seen.*'

""We view Him, whom no eye can see,

With faith's keen vision stedfastly.""

In this confidence they set sail; nor did they suffer themselves to be confounded by any of the unspeakable difficulties of the following years, till they and we at last beheld the completion of what they hoped for in faith.

They sailed by Shetland, April 22nd; and, after an expeditious and agreeable voyage, entered Davis's Straits in the beginning of May. Here they encountered a field of floating ice, while enveloped in a thick fog; but the next day a terrible storm arose, which dispersed the ice and freed them at the same time from their fears. On the 13th they came in sight of the coast of Greenland, when a violent tempest of four days' continuance, preceded by a total eclipse of the sun, drove them back more than sixty leagues. May 20th, they cast anchor in Ball's River, after a voyage of six weeks; and joyfully welcomed the snowy cliffs and savage inhabitants of a country which had so long been the chief object of their wishes. The word of the day was, *The peace of God, which passeth all understanding, shall keep your hearts and minds through Jesus Christ.* By this they were frequently encouraged to a peaceful and believing perseverance, during the first ensuing years, amidst all the oppositions which they met with, and the slender prospect they entertained of the conversion of the heathen.

The sight of the first Greenlanders, though they could not speak a word to them, was accompanied with sensations of lively pleasure; their pitiable condition pierced them to the heart, and they prayed the Lord, *the Light to enlighten the gentiles*, that he would grant them grace, wisdom, and power, to bring some of them at least out of darkness into His marvellous light. Immediately on their landing they repaired to Mr. Egede. He gave them a cordial reception, congratulated them on their undertaking, and promised them his assistance in learning the language. They next fixed on a spot for their building, on the nearest habitable part of the coast, to which they afterward gave the name of New Hernnhutt; and having consecrated it with prayer began to run up a Greenland hut of stones and sods, in which they might find shelter, until they had erected a wooden house. At first the natives regarded them with contempt, concluding from the readiness with which they engaged in every kind of manual labour, that they were the Factor's servants; and being scattered among the islands and hills to fish, catch seals, and hunt deer, while in winter they made journies on sledges to their acquaintance upwards of a hundred leagues North or South; the Brethren had little access to them, and but faint hopes of making any permanent impression on their minds in their wandering mode of existence. Some of the natives, however, paid a visit to them, but it was only from curiosity to see their buildings, or to beg needles, fish hooks, knives, and other such articles, if not to steal; and no proffered advantages could tempt them to remain for a short time at the Settlement. Till at length when they understood that the object of these faithful, tried, and persevering Missionaries was not to trade with them, but to make them acquainted with their Creator; and when they observed their modest and gentle carriage, so different from that of other Europeans, they paid them more attention, pressed them to come to their huts, and promised to return the visit themselves. A more frequent intercourse gradually commenced, and the Greenlanders would sometimes spend a night with the Brethren. The motives of their visits were, indeed, glaringly selfish. They wanted either food and shelter, or presents of needles and other things. They even bluntly declared, that if the Missionaries would give them no stock-fish, they would no longer listen to what they had to say: and during the winter, which was intensely cold, the Brethren could not refuse their request for provisions. They did not altogether discontinue their visits in summer, but they generally came after spending the night in feasting and revelling, too drowsy to support a conversation, or intent only upon hearing some news, or on begging or purloining whatever might strike their fancy. Their pilfering habits made their visits not a little troublesome to the Brethren, but the latter did not wish to frighten them away; and were content for the present, that they came at all, especially as a few of them discovered a satisfaction in being present at the evening meetings, though held in German, and made inquiries into the design of them. After a series of trying hardships; and after enduring privations for years, they were encouraged in their mission, established in much long-suffering and patience, by one of the natives visiting them, and desiring to ""see their things."" They showed him what they had, supposing that he wished to barter some Greenland food for their iron ware. But after remaining quite silent for some time, he at last said that he had been with the Minister, (Mr. Egede) who had told him wonderful things of *One*, who was said to have created heaven and earth, and was called God. Did they know any thing about it? If they did, they should tell him something more, as he had forgotten a good deal. This discourse made a deep impression on their minds. They told him of the creation of man, and the intention it; of the fall and consequent corruption of the human race; of the redemption through Christ; of the resurrection; and of eternal happiness and damnation. The poor Greenlander listened very attentively, was present at their evening meeting, and slept all night in their tent. Further inquiries were afterwards made among the natives, till the Brethren had their two Greenland houses completely filled, and a native congregation collected. The word of the gospel was eventually propagated by the Missionaries through a vast extent of country, and its glad tidings spread still farther by the savages themselves, so that a numerous company of Greenlanders have been gathered to Jesus Christ by the preaching of his word—moulded into a spiritual congregation by the operation of the Holy Ghost (says the above historian,) and furnished with such provisions for its good discipline, both within and without, that amidst all defects, it might in truth be called a living, flourishing, fruit-bearing plant of the heavenly Father's planting.

Such an example of success in Missionary exertions, in the frozen and uncultivated regions of Greenland and of Labrador, as the United Brethren have set, holds out every encouragement to hope that a mission would succeed among the Esquimaux at Hudson's Bay. They resemble the Greenlanders in their aspect, dress, and mode of living; and speaking the same language, it would greatly aid the mission to them, if one or two Christian natives could be obtained and prevailed upon to join it from the coast of Greenland. They are shouting from their native rocks for instruction, and have appealed to the Christian sympathy and benevolence of every friend of missions, in language of the same import as the call of Macedonia,—""We want to know the grand God.""

""Shall we, whose souls are lighted

With wisdom from on high,

Shall we to men benighted

The lamp of life deny?

Salvation! oh, salvation!
The joyful sound proclaim,
Till each remotest nation
Has learn'd Messiah's name.
Waft, waft, ye winds, his story,
And you, ye waters, roll,
Till, like a sea of glory,
It spreads from pole to pole;
Till o'er our ransomed nature,
The Lamb for sinners slain,
Redeemer, King, Creator!
In bliss returns to reign.""
Bishop of Calcutta.

The 5th.—Sunday. The wind has blown hard all day, so as to permit, from the rolling of the ship, of my only reading the Morning and Evening Prayers, for divine worship. I know that God, who made heaven, earth, and seas, is not confined to forms of prayer, how ever excellent, any more than to temples made with hands. But as a formulary, how full and comprehensive is that of the Church of England! and how well adapted to express the feelings of the mind, humbled, and penitentially exercised, yet exalted in hope at the throne of a covenant God in Christ Jesus. When the prayers are *prayed*, and not merely read in the cold formality of office, instead of wearying the mind by repetition, how often are they the means of arresting our wandering thoughts, and awakening a devotional feeling! This effect, I trust, was produced in our minds, as we met together, for the public services of the day, in the cabin of the ship.

From the 5th to the 9th, we had stiff gales of wind from the same quarter, which caused the sea to roll with a majesty and grandeur that I never before witnessed. I stood on the quarterdeck, in admiration of the scene, and of the wonders of God in the deep, as wave rolled after wave, occasionally breaking on its *mountainous* top into a roaring and foaming surge. But while the waves roar and the winds howl around me, I am borne in safety through the mighty waters towards the desired haven. What a fit emblem is this experience of the spiritual and eternal safety of the Christian, in the ark of the covenant, amidst the foaming billows of affliction, the wind of temptation, and every storm of trial raised by man in a fallen and disordered world, branded with so many marks of its Creator's displeasure.

We were prevented from meeting in the cabin, for divine service, on Sunday the 12th, from its blowing a hard gale, and the violent tossing of the ship. We now experienced a sensible alteration in the weather, as being much milder; and a couple of black wolves and a bear, which we had on board, were evidently affected by the change of the atmosphere, as we were bearing up for the Orkney Isles. On the 15th, we anchored in Stromness harbour, and, leaving this anchorage on the 17th, we reached Yarmouth Roads, October the 23d; and through a kind protecting Providence, I landed, on the following day, from the ship, in the Thames.

Since my departure from England, in May 1820, to this period of my return, not one accident have I met with, nor have I been called to experience a single day's illness. Though in perils oft by land and by sea, and exposed to threatened dangers of the ice, and of the desert, still my life has been preserved.

Praised be the Lord God of my salvation!

In sending this volume to the press, I feel that I am discharging a duty which I owe to the natives of the rocks and of the wilderness, whom I have seen in the darkness and misery of heathenism; and I ardently desire that the Mission already entered upon, may become the means of widely extending the knowledge of Christianity among them. I have no higher wish in life, than to spend and be spent in the service of Christ, for the salvation of the North American Indians. Not my will, however, but His be done, who alone can direct and control all Missions successfully, to the fulfilment of His prophetic word, when ""The wilderness shall become a fruitful field,"" and ""the desert shall rejoice and blossom as the rose.""

Since the foregoing sheets were sent to the Printer, very gratifying intelligence has been received of the improved state of the Colony; and a sanguine hope is entertained that several native Indian children from different nations will be added to the number of those already upon the Church Mission School establishment at the Red River.

THE END.

Footnotes

1
So called from the junction of the Assiniboine River with the Red River.
2
1 Corin. vii. 12.
3
Gen. ii. 24.
4
Without blame.
5
Between Catholics and Heritics.
6
See Captain Franklin's Journey to the Coppermine River, Vol. II. p. 270, second edition.
7
There is no salvation beyond the pale of the Roman Church.
8
Since my return to England I have been favoured with the following communication from a gentleman, who travelled in Siberia, to promote the object of the British and Foreign Bible Society, in the general circulation of the Scriptures; and which-corroborates the above report. "The Russians have made many proselytes to the Greek Church, (he observes,) from among the natives of the North-West coast of North America, and two different supplies of copies of the Scriptures in the Slavonian and modern Russ languages have been forwarded to that quarter, for the use of their settlements there, by the Russian Bible Society."